SAVAGE

Claudio Macor

SAVAGE

OBERON BOOKS
LONDON

WWW.OBERONBOOKS.COM

First published in 2016 by Oberon Books Ltd
521 Caledonian Road, London N7 9RH
Tel: +44 (0) 20 7607 3637 / Fax: +44 (0) 20 7607 3629
e-mail: info@oberonbooks.com
www.oberonbooks.com

A catalogue record for this book is available from the British
Library.

PB ISBN: 9781783197798
E ISBN: 9781783197804

Cover design and Graphic design: Rob Cook

Visit www.oberonbooks.com to read more about all our books
and to buy them. You will also find features, author interviews and
news of any author events, and you can sign up for e-newsletters
so that you're always first to hear about our new releases.

FOREWORD

This important, valuable play sheds a light on the Danish doctor, Carl Peter Værnet, who believed that he had found the 'cure' for homosexuality and who experimented on gay concentration camp prisoners. His fervent belief tallied with the homophobic persecution policies of the Nazis, who sought to eradicate what they called 'abnormal existence' (homosexuality). My 1998-99 campaign to expose Værnet triggered a public outcry in Denmark, where most people had been unaware of his crimes and the high-level measures taken to shield him from prosecution. The Danish government passed the buck; referring me to their National Archives. They suggested that I conduct my own investigation and initiate a private prosecution. I was told the archive papers on Værnet were classified until 2025. But faced with mounting public, media and parliamentary pressure, the Danish government eventually relented. Access was given to the previously top secret files. They revealed Værnet's medical Nazism, his protection by postwar Danish state and inaction by Allied war crime prosecutors. The Danish authorities have yet to explain why they shielded him nor have the Danish and British governments apologised for allowing a Nazi war criminal to get off scott-free.

Peter Tatchell, human rights campaigner.

AUTHOR BIOGRAPHY

Claudio was born in South Africa to Italian parents, after abandoning his acting career he moved to London in 1983 where he began writing plays. For the stage his credits include *Savage, Zanetto, The Tailor-Made Man* (London and off-Broadway), *In The Dead of Night, The End of Innocence, Santa Cruz, The Other Man,* Stage adaptation of Gabriele D'Annunzio's classsic novel *L'Innocente, The Man Inside, The Love of An Angel, Casanova* and *Venetian Heat. The Tailor-Made Man* has been adapted into a Radio play and a New Musical. Screenplays include *The Tailor-Made Man, In The Dead* of *Night* and *Out of the Night.*

ACKNOWLEDGMENTS

Andrea Leoncini, Chris Hislop (PR), Gianni Leoncini, Janet Glass, Roy Tan, Daniel McCarroll, Matthew Kiziltan, William De Coverley, Tom Holloway, Louise Nicolson, Jamie Eastlake, Nick Hayes, Roman Grey, Suzy Bastone, Alex Reece, Brian Hook, Louis Hartshorn, Moira O'Connell, Edmund Attill, Laurel Dougall, Peter Tatchell and the Peter Tatchell Foundation.

The first production of *SAVAGE* was produced by Andrea Leoncini for LWL Entertainment Ltd with the first performance on the 1 July 2016 at the Arts Theatre London, with the following cast and creative team:

The Cast:

NIKOLAI BERGSEN	ALEXANDER HUETSON
ZACK TRAVIS	NIC KYLE
ILSE PAULSEN	EMILY LYNNE
OBERGRUPPENFHURER GENERAL /HEINRICH VON AESCHELMAN	BRADLEY CLARKSON
GEORG JENSEN	LEE KNIGHT
MAJOR HEMINGWAY/ GUARD/FREUDE/PRESENTER	CHRISTOPHER HINES
FREDERICH/GORAN/ RODRIGO/DETMER	KRISTIAN SIMEONOV
AND DOCTOR CARL PETER VÆRNET	GARY FANNIN

Creative Team:

DIRECTED BY:	CLAUDIO MACOR
ORIGINAL MUSIC COMPOSED BY:	SALVATORE DE CONCILIS
CHOREOGRAPHED BY:	ADAM SCOWN
DESIGNED BY:	DAVID SHIELDS
COSTUMES DESIGNED BY:	JAMIE ATTLE
PHOTOGRAPHY BY:	ROY TAN
COVER DESIGN AND GRAPHIC DESIGN BY:	ROB COOK

Characters

NIKOLAI BERGSEN

ZACK TRAVIS

ILSE PAULSEN

OBERGRUPPENFUHRER GENERAL/
HEINRICH VON AESCHELMAN

GEORG JENSEN

MAJOR HEMINGWAY/GUARD/FREUDE/PRESENTER

FREDRICH/GORAN/RODRIGO/DETMER

And

DOCTOR CARL PETER VÆRNET

PLAYWRIGHT'S NOTE

To try to tamper with nature is doomed to fail. Nature forms part of a balanced world that presents the truth and not choices.

It has often said that certain characteristics and lifestyles are choices when in fact choice plays no part at all.

Fear of the unknown and ignorance leads to anger, wild irrational behaviour and cruelty.

To be able to heal a fellow human being is a noble profession, a vocation like no other. It is only when that medical knowledge is used to enhance a particular person's personal beliefs that it's bound to fail.

When discrimination is whispered behind closed doors is when it's at its most dangerous. Practised out in the open it's when it's most cruel. Given the support, backing and encouragement of the state is when it's simply SAVAGE.

During the tumultuous times of the SECOND WORLD WAR people's lives were disrupted and scattered across time and place.

COPENHAGEN 1940 and 1945

MALMO 1946

BUENOS AIRES, ARGENTINA 1947

Dedicated to ANDREA x

ACT ONE

A member of the Royal Danish Medical Association addresses the audience.

PRESENTER: Good day Gentlemen. *(Looks around.)* Very good! Thank you for attending this special general meeting as requested by Doctor Carl Peter Værnet. The floor is all yours Doctor.

(There is no applause just some rumbling chat. The member of the Royal Danish Medical Association exits as DOCTOR CARL PETER VÆRNET, 30-40s, walks into in a single, harsh white light. He's a plain-looking man with insignificant features and slick back hair; however there is a sharp, piercing glint in his eye. He looks around at his audience, clears his throat and speaks.)

VÆRNET: Thank you and thank you to the Royal Danish Medical Association for allowing me this opportunity to address you. *(Beat.)* I have been a member of the association for over ten years and my hormone therapy research has been generously funded and applauded. I have made great strides in micro short wave treatments of cancer and other diseases. Three years ago I became a member of the Danish Nationalist Socialists, since then my funding has been cut and my general practice has diminished considerably. I don't stand before you asking for handouts but to urge you to support me in a new vital treatment for a disease that is threatening the very fibre of the Danish nation. *(Beat.)* It's the question of homosexuality. *(Beat.)* It can no longer be accepted that what happens in private remains private, all things which take place in the sexual sphere are not the private affair of the individual but signify the life and death of our nation. Therefore we must be absolutely

11

clear, that if we continue to have this burden in Denmark, that will be the end of our Danish ways.

We cannot simply rip them out like weeds and throw them onto a heap and burn them nor can we imprison them because when the homosexual comes out of prison he's still a homosexual. *(Beat.)* Their theory is that it's not a choice, that it's natural, such a theory is misguided and propaganda.

(Pause.)

The Third Reich has joined our great nation without destroying our cities or towns, nor have they killed us in vast numbers. Germany is not a land full of barbarians instead it's the land of Beethoven, Schiller, Goethe and Wagner, we should be honoured they have come to help and guide us therefore we cannot disappointment them. To achieve a clean and pure new world order we must eradicate the homosexual from Dublin to Vladivostok. *(Beat.)* The solution is my new hormone therapy. To cure an individual is to eliminate the disease completely so that the good blood and the increasingly healthy blood we are cultivating in Denmark will be kept pure. With your support and kind patronage I will prove to you that my new, radical, hormone therapy is an effective CURE of homosexuality and WILL be successful. Thank you.

(As the light on DOCTOR VÆRNET softens, he exits full of pomp and self-importance. Jazz music starts to play in the background. Smoke fills the room.)

*** *** ***

THE CORNER LIGHT CLUB.

The club is a dark underground establishment frequented by a bohemian crowd. The club is dimly lit and has a couple of chairs to one side. Waiters set the table and mingle as NIKOLAI BERGSEN, 30s and ZACK TRAVIS, 30s enter and sit. Both men are handsome and immaculately dressed in their elegant suits. Their refined demeanour and good looks would not be out of place in a fashion magazine. NIKOLAI is Danish and ZACK is American. DETMER, 20s, enters and serves them Champagne cocktails. He kisses them both on the cheek as if he knows them well. He's a performer, handsome, sexy and scantily clad. The stage is not a specific raised area instead it's just a random area of the club. DETMER dresses the chair with a small perfume style bottle and a face cloth. His movements are as if in a dream. Hushed conversations are heard but the clientele is not visible as the lighting and dark recesses hide them. The lights darken further, the conversations die out; a palatable sense of anticipation is in the air. A spotlight shines brightly over the chair. The music fades as the club falls silent. GEORG JENSEN, 30s, walks into the light. The audience's applause is a roar of whistles and whooping. He is in full drag as DEE DEE SAHARAH. NIKOLAI and ZACK smile, laugh and NIKOLAI reaches over and takes ZACK's hand. They enjoy being there. GEORG's get up is outrageous, a huge wig, oversized eyelashes, full colourful make-up, jungle red lipstick and a voluminous gown complete his impressive, outlandish appearance.

(DEE DEE SAHARAH takes to the stage and savours the attention. Throughout her act DETMER assists her.

She raises her arms slightly and the audience exuberance falls silent. Music plays as DEE DEE starts to sing 'LILI MARLENE.' What DEE DEE is about to create is a reversal! As she sings the song she removes her entire drag get-up.

The gloves, wig, make-up, shoes, gown, GEORG removes DEE DEE SAHARA to revert back into a man wearing only his underpants. Music interludes give time to allow the transformation. All discarded items are picked up off the floor by DETMER.)

DEE DEE: Underneath the lantern by the barrack gate,
                Darling I remember the way you used to wait.

   (DEE DEE removes her gloves.)

DEE DEE: Twas there that you whispered tenderly, that you loved me. You'd always be my Lili of the lamplight, my own Lili Marlene.

(DEE DEE removes her wig and scalp cap.)

DEE DEE: Time would come for roll call, time for us to part.

(She removes her eyelashes.)

DEE DEE: Darling I'd caress you and press you to my heart.

(She unzips her dress and lets it fall to the floor, revealing a corset and stockings.)

DEE DEE: And there 'neath that far off lantern light, I'd hold you tight, we'd kiss goodnight my Lili of the lamplight; my own Lili Marlene.

(She removes her shoes and kicks them away.)

DEE DEE: Orders came for sailing somewhere over there; all confined to barracks was more than I could bear.

(She removes her corset and stockings.)

DEE DEE: I knew you were waiting in the street; I heard your feet but could not meet My Lili of the lamplight; my own Lili Marlene.

(She removes her false nails.)

DEE DEE: Resting in a billet just behind the line, even though we're parted your lips are close to mine.

(For the rest of the song DEE DEE SAHARA removes her make-up. She picks up the little bottle that contains olive oil and dabs the cloth and starts to smear away the make-up.)

DEE DEE: You wait where that lantern softly gleams; your sweet face seems to haunt my dreams, my Lili of the lamplight, my own Lili Marlene.

(The transformation is complete. DEE DEE SAHARA is no more instead GEORG stands proud as a man, his face smudged by make-up and naked except for his underpants. DETMER recedes into the dark and out of sight. GEORG takes hold of the song.)

DEE DEE: When we are marching in the mud and cold
                and when my rucksack seems more than I
                can hold, my love for you renews my might,
                I'm warm again, my sack is light, it's you Lili
                Marlene, it's you Lili Marlene …

(NIKOLAI and ZACK start applauding but GEORG raises his arms, before the audience can react. He's emotional, sad.)

GEORG: No, don't applaud, don't say a word. Dee Dee
                Sahara is going away, but she will be back. I
                promise. Now it's Georg that must face the
                world, a world so uncertain, so mad, I can't
                stay here. Tonight the Corner Light Club will
                close; it has been my joy; my life, that is why
                I'm protecting it. Denmark belongs to Nazi
                Germany now … *(His voice breaks.)* Be strong,
                be safe, my wonderful people out there in the
                dark …

(Through tears he sings …)

GEORG: When we are marching in the mud and cold,
                and when my rucksack seems more than I
                can hold, my love for you renews my might,
                I'm warm again, my sack is light, it's you Lili
                Marlene, it's you ….

(As GEORG finishes the song the lights change, the music slowly fades as NIKOLAI and ZACK get up and walk away. GEORG exits into the dark

DETMER hands them their light overcoats. ZACK puts his on as NIKOLAI looks back deep in his thoughts.

The lights change, darken as the night air bites. ZACK puts his arm around NIKOLAI as they wonder outside. NIKOLAI looks around.)

NIKOLAI: The stars are bright tonight.

ZACK:	*(Looks up.)* Yeah. *(NIKOLAI can't stop staring at the sky.)* Do you want to go for another drink?
NIKOLAI:	Where?
ZACK:	Bjorn is selling drinks at his home.
NIKOLAI:	He's an idiot; he'll get caught and thrown into prison.
ZACK:	Well we can't stay out in the cold.
NIKOLAI:	I'm not cold.
ZACK:	Are you going home?
NIKOLAI:	What for?
ZACK:	Ah … because that's where you live.
NIKOLAI:	No.
ZACK:	What then?
NIKOLAI:	Just want to walk.
ZACK:	We look suspicious.
NIKOLAI:	There's no law against walking.

(They wander aimlessly.)

ZACK:	Georg will be back.
NIKOLAI:	Sure he will.
ZACK:	Is that's what's upsetting you?
NIKOLAI:	When Georg switched off the lights it was as if my life was snuffed out.
ZACK:	They're talking about curfews now.
NIKOLAI:	I don't want to huddle in shadows.
ZACK:	The sun will shine again.

(They wander under a street light.)

NIKOLAI:	We met in the Corner Light Club.

ZACK: That wasn't difficult, you were always there.

NIKOLAI: No I wasn't.

ZACK: Come on, sure you were.

NIKOLAI: Well you were hardly a stranger.

ZACK: It was a Saturday.

NIKOLAI: Friday.

ZACK: The 7th.

NIKOLAI: The 24th.

ZACK: The 24th was when you let me stay.

NIKOLAI: That was a mistake.

ZACK: *(ZACK grabs his head.)* You bastard!

NIKOLAI: We met on Friday the 7th.

ZACK: April.

NIKOLAI: May.

ZACK: What difference does a few days make?

NIKOLAI: It's been nearly two years.

ZACK: *(Teases.)* Poor you.

NIKOLAI: I deserve the Nobel Prize for putting up with you.

ZACK: You deserve to get your ass out of the cold.

NIKOLAI: You Yanks are all soft; you know nothing about the cold.

ZACK: We can't all be born in an icebox.

NIKOLAI: I'm going to miss Georg.

ZACK: He'll still be around.

    (Pause.)

NIKOLAI: Why did he choose that song?

17

ZACK:	All the soldiers are signing it now.
NIKOLAI:	I should be a soldier.
ZACK:	You didn't pass the medical remember.
NIKOLAI:	And you have diplomatic immunity.
ZACK:	Only until America joins the war.
NIKOLAI:	What? Will they close the Embassy?
ZACK:	I'm only a secretary; I'll be the first to be sent home.
NIKOLAI:	Talk about bad timing.
ZACK:	Whenever is it perfect timing?
NIKOLAI:	People should be left to live their lives, allowed to plan …
ZACK:	Plans have a habit of falling apart.
NIKOLAI:	The Germans have been here for months and nothing is happening, why don't they just leave.
ZACK:	Denmark is just a stepping-stone.
NIKOLAI:	To where?
ZACK:	Norway.
NIKOLAI:	Then go to Norway, leave us alone.
ZACK:	We must lie low, we can't do anything rash. They're everywhere watching.
NIKOLAI:	I refuse to hide.
ZACK:	Just lie low.

(Pause.)

NIKOLAI:	Will you leave me behind?
ZACK:	I've laid out a plan to bring you with me.
NIKOLAI:	As what, a stowaway???

ZACK: A refugee.

NIKOLAI: That's so humiliating.

ZACK: It ain't gonna be easy.

NIKOLAI: Sure it is you can go back to Washington, find a quarter back, meet him behind the locker room; forget Europe.

ZACK: You're such an ass sometimes.

NIKOLAI: Am I?

ZACK: I love you, how can I leave you.

NIKOLAI: Love has nothing to do with it.

ZACK: Sure it has.

NIKOLAI: Why did it have to change? Copenhagen was so open and free. Urrgh it gets me so mad!!!

ZACK: Working at the American Embassy has its benefits.

(Pause.)

NIKOLAI: Nice thought though.

ZACK: What is?

NIKOLAI: Running away together.

ZACK: You're such a romantic.

NIKOLAI: What's wrong with that?

ZACK: Nothing.

NIKOLAI: Is it cold in Washington?

ZACK: Not like here.

NIKOLAI: Yeah but our summers are hot.

ZACK: Hot? Are you kidding? Anything above 22 degrees and you guys melt.

(NIKOLAI laughs.)

NIKOLAI: What's Washington like?

ZACK: Big.

NIKOLAI: Everything is big in America.

ZACK: Full of government buildings …

NIKOLAI: Sounds boring.

ZACK: Let's not talk about Washington until we have to.

NIKOLAI: Okay.

ZACK: I'm not going anywhere, not for a while.

NIKOLAI: That's not your decision. *(Smiles.)* You'd look great as a Marine.

ZACK: Keep your fantasies to yourself.

NIKOLAI: I never told you.

ZACK: Told me what?

NIKOLAI: How excited I was when we first met.

ZACK: So was I.

NIKOLAI: The club was full of smoke; Georg had telephones on all the tables. I dialled your code, you answered and I asked you over. Watching you walk towards me, it was like in slow motion, the smoke parted and all I could see was your naughty, mischievous smile.

ZACK: You said the dumbest thing.

NIKOLAI: What?

ZACK: Can I cook you dinner?

NIKOLAI: That wasn't dumb.

ZACK: Sure it was.

NIKOLAI: I meant; I wanted to keep you until dinner, the following night.

(ZACK is touched.)

ZACK: I stayed for five days.

NIKOLAI: Not so dumb after all, huh.

ZACK: No, not at all.

(ZACK sees a dark doorway.)

ZACK: Come here.

(ZACK pulls NIKOLAI towards him.)

NIKOLAI: A stolen kiss in a darkened doorway? I feel like Garbo.

ZACK: Garbo is prettier.

(NIKOLAI smacks him gently. ZACK pretends he's hurt. They lark about.)

NIKOLAI: My home is all warm and cosy.

ZACK: I need get back to the Embassy. I'm out late way too often.

NIKOLAI: No one will notice you're gone.

ZACK: Everyone is watching these days.

NIKOLAI: You're only a secretary, remember.

(ZACK moves away.)

ZACK: Bashing away at the typewriter all day, sending dispatches trying to second-guess what the Nazis are going to do next; when all the time I'm thinking of ways to leave, to find a safer place. You are not a casual encounter. I know twenty months is not a very long time but we're together; I want us to be there, old, cranky and getting on each other's nerves. I want all that with you.

NIKOLAI: We're two men, remember?

ZACK: I don't see that.

NIKOLAI: You'll have to do a magic trick with your
            Ambassador.

ZACK: I'll trick him any way I can.

NIKOLAI: It's the only way to rescue me.

ZACK: I have to ….

NIKOLAI: and take me back to Connecticut meet all your
            Harvard chums.

ZACK: I'd rather be here with you surrounded by all
            your art and history.

NIKOLAI: You Yanks have only been around five minutes.

ZACK: We can't all be as ancient as you.

(NIKOLAI takes ZACK by his lapels and pulls him towards into a darker light and kisses him. Quite rough at first but then it becomes softer, gentler. They continue to kiss as they speak, it's as if they are saying goodbye, or the last kiss. There is an urgency, a sadness, about their embrace.)

NIKOLAI: I love you.

ZACK: Yes.

NIKOLAI: No matter what …

ZACK: I'll never forget …

NIKOLAI: It's just you …

(ZACK kisses him passionately. The night air is cold, crisp, still. The breeze picks up as they cling to each other. Suddenly large searchlights are switched on as a screeching siren rings out across the night air.

NIKOLAI and ZACK break and try to run away in terror when a group of Nazis surround them. The lights are blinding and disorientating.

NIKOLAI and ZACK freeze; they stare at the advancing soldiers. NIKOLAI attempts to escape, ZACK holds him back. The Nazis are closing in menacing, intimidating, as they are about to grab NIKOLAI and ZACK.

BLACK OUT.)

***   ***   ***

DOCTOR CARL PETER VÆRNET'S SURGERY. COPENHAGEN.

ILSE PAULSEN, 20s, enters. She is quite pretty but with her hair severely pulled back and her pristine nurse's uniform she has a functional yet stern appearance. She carries a metal tray. She places it on a chair and starts to pull out the doctor's bed with straps, ready for examination. She positions it across the back. She rolls out a hospital screen on wheels. It has three panels of fabric on a metal frame. Next she positions a hospital trolley next to the bed. She takes the tray and puts it on the trolley and proceeds to arrange all the surgical instruments on it. There is no sterilization basin. ILSE makes sure all the instruments are neatly aligned. The setting is clinical and eerily gruesome. DOCTOR CARL PETER VÆRNET enters. His white coat covers his suit. ILSE does not say a word as DOCTOR VÆRNET inspects the instruments.

VÆRNET: What time is it?

ILSE: *(Checks her nurse's watch pinned to her uniform.)* Ten thirty.

VÆRNET: Is there any word he'll be late.

ILSE: No.

VÆRNET: Good.

(Pause.)

ILSE: Do you want me to stay?

VÆRNET: Of course, why wouldn't you?

ILSE: I thought you may want to be alone with …

VÆRNET: I have nothing to hide.

ILSE: Very well.

(DOCTOR VÆRNET is anxious. ILSE is stoic in her silence. An uncomfortable silence fills the surgery.)

VÆRNET: What time is it?

ILSE: *(Looks at her watch.)* Ten thirty-one.

VÆRNET: Yes … of course …

(Silence.)

ILSE: Did you sleep well?

VÆRNET: Not a wink …

ILSE: Too excited.

VÆRNET: And nervous.

ILSE: Nothing to be nervous about, you are a great doctor with an impeccable reputation.

VÆRNET: And very few patients.

ILSE: Doctors are expensive; people make do with homemade remedies now.

VÆRNET: Quacks have ruined the profession, they serve up lethal concoctions.

ILSE: Perhaps but it gives people comfort.

VÆRNET: There is no comfort in prescribing some poisonous mixture.

ILSE: Why don't you reduce your costs to attract more patients?

VÆRNET: If the Royal Danish Medical Association subsidised my research then my circumstances would be very different.

ILSE: It was only a suggestion.

VÆRNET: My therapies are not some silly pill you take when you have a headache; they are expertly researched, experimented upon to achieve the right balance. All this takes a very long time to perfect and a great deal of investment.

ILSE: I'm trying to secure your future.

VÆRNET: I know you are and I appreciate your concern.

ILSE: Thank you.

(ILSE turns away and pretends to adjust the instruments. DOCTOR VÆRNET fiddles with his tie; he starts to sweat and feels irritated and uncomfortable. He moves away. FREDERICH, 20s, a young very good-looking Nazi soldier enters with NIKOLAI. FREDERICH's uniform and clean-cut look are immaculate. NIKOLAI has his arm around FREDERICH shoulder, he's been beaten and his face is bruised. The guards have removed his coat and tie and he looks dishevelled. DOCTOR VÆRNET turns to them.)

VÆRNET: Put him there.

(FREDERICH dumps NIKOLAI on the chair. NIKOLAI touches his face.)

VÆRNET: Thank you, I'll call if I need you.

FREDERICH: Yes, Herr Doctor. *(He salutes and exits.)*

(VÆRNET looks at him with disdain.)

NIKOLAI: Where am I?

(No answer.)

NIKOLAI: Who are you?

(No answer.)

NIKOLAI: What is this place?

(Pause.)

VÆRNET: What is your name?

NIKOLAI: Why am I here?

VÆRNET: You're here to answer, not question! What is your name?

NIKOLAI: *(Confused.)* What?

VÆRNET: Name, you must have a name?

NIKOLAI: Nikolai Bergsen.

VÆRNET: Bergsen, a good Danish name.

NIKOLAI: What do you want?

VÆRNET:	What were you doing out in the street late at night?
NIKOLAI:	Walking.
VÆRNET:	Why?
NIKOLAI:	I needed air.
VÆRNET:	Alone?
NIKOLAI:	Yes.
VÆRNET:	Lies.
NIKOLAI:	It was late, I was walking home.
VÆRNET:	In the wrong direction.
NIKOLAI:	How do you know in which direction I live?
VÆRNET:	Why were you out late at night?
NIKOLAI:	As I said, I needed air.
VÆRNET:	You can get air from an open window.
NIKOLAI:	Who are you? What do you want?
VÆRNET:	You.
NIKOLAI:	Look, I don't know why they arrested me. I've done nothing wrong.
VÆRNET:	Haven't you?
NIKOLAI:	No, nothing, I swear.
VÆRNET:	I say you have!
NIKOLAI:	I'm a normal ordinary person. I work in the art gallery, keep my head down and don't bother anyone. I don't understand why I'm here talking to someone I have no idea who you are.
VÆRNET:	I'm Doctor Carl Værnet.
NIKOLAI:	I don't need a doctor.
VÆRNET:	That is for me to decide.

NIKOLAI: This is all a mistake, can I go home now please.

VÆRNET: I've yet to determine if it's a mistake or not.

NIKOLAI: I must inform my boss about what's happened; he's expecting me at the gallery.

(Pause.)

VÆRNET: The other person has been sent home.

NIKOLAI: *(Flinches.)* ah … who?

VÆRNET: The man you were with.

NIKOLAI: There was no other man.

VÆRNET: He's an American diplomat, works at the Embassy. They couldn't arrest him.

NIKOLAI: I told you I was out alone getting some air.

(NIKOLAI gets up and makes to move.)

VÆRNET: *(LOUD.)* Sit down!!!

NIKOLAI: *(Sits. Pause and looks around. To ILSE.)* Who's that?

VÆRNET: My assistant.

(NIKOLAI looks away. Fear sets in. DOCTOR VÆRNET walks passed him without looking at him, making NIKOLAI feel very uncomfortable.)

ILSE: Is there anything you need Doctor?

VÆRNET: No. Thank you.

ILSE: Very well.

(Pause.)

VÆRNET: Are you or have you ever been a homosexual?

NIKOLAI: What?

VÆRNET: *(Shouts.)* Answer the question.

NIKOLAI:	It is too personal to warrant an answer.
VÆRNET:	Why were you walking around at night?
NIKOLAI:	I told you …
VÆRNET:	No you didn't, but I'll tell you; you were out on the streets, looking for men.
NIKOLAI:	That is not true.
VÆRNET:	It is true; you were seen leaving the Corner Light Club a cesspool of corrupt vice. I've been trying to get the authorities to close it down for years but they find grown men dressed as women amusing. *(Beat.)* They've been watching you for a while now.
NIKOLAI:	Who's watching?
VÆRNET:	Men coming and going, collars turned up, trying to disguise your faces, always lurking in the dark.
NIKOLAI:	You have a fertile imagination Doctor.
VÆRNET:	You used to frequent that place often, and you returned last night. *(Snaps.)* What were you doing there?
NIKOLAI:	Enjoying a Champagne cocktail.
VÆRNET:	And meeting men.
NIKOLAI:	May I remind you Doctor, that homosexuality has been legal in Denmark since 1933 and what adults do in private is of no concern of yours.
VÆRNET:	Adults yes but homosexuality is a disease that must be cured.
NIKOLAI:	It's as natural as a rose is a rose.
VÆRNET:	*(Gets louder.)* It's an evil that destroys lives.
NIKOLAI:	That is something I've never seen.

(DOCTOR VÆRNET is engulfed with rage and bitterness.)

VÆRNET: Growing up in Skagen, a remote town way up north, I clung to the few friends I had and in particular Carsten. We were at school together enjoyed digging up slugs, fighting in the snow, pretending to be in love with the girls one day and scaring them with spiders the next. It was a happy normal childhood. We were both good at school so there was never any rivalry but children grow, they develop personalities, likes and dislikes. It upset me when we started to drift apart, I couldn't understand it, had I done something wrong? He became bitter and nasty. I pleaded with him to tell me what was wrong; finally he confessed he had feelings for other boys, that he had caught the disease, a disease so sly as not to be visible and so manipulative to force you to do things you wouldn't dare do. I tried to help him but to no avail, his feelings grew stronger and so was his shame, a shame that consumed him. He attended Church more often, prayed for a miracle but terrified to confess to the priest. He became ever more desperate and isolated. I didn't know what to say to him, I told him God did not make him like this, that he was sick, that he should see a doctor, but there was no one to talk to, to seek help. *(Pause.)* I found him in the outside toilet, head down; drowned in excrement. I pulled him out, screamed for help as I held him. His end symbolised his feelings. *(Pause.)* I never cried; I couldn't, instead a rage burned inside of me. I knew a cure had to be found.

NIKOLAI: A rose is still a rose.

(DOCTOR VÆRNET looks at him.)

VÆRNET: I ask you again, are you or have you ever been a homosexual?

NIKOLAI: And I repeat my answer. What's private should remain private.

(DOCTOR VÆRNET understands. He goes to the exit, looks out, nods his head and returns to ILSE. NIKOLAI looks around; the silence is full of menace and fear. A GUARD enters and announces OBERGRUPPENFUHRER GENERAL HEINRICH VON AESCHELMAN.)

GUARD: Obergruppenfuhrer General Heinrich Von Aeschelman.

(DOCTOR VÆRNET stands upright while ILSE looks away slightly not wanting to show her fear. OBERGRUPPENFUHRER HEINRICH VON AESCHLEMAN enters followed by a FREDERICH who is always on hand. DOCTOR VÆRNET salutes him proudly.)

VÆRNET: Heil Hitler.

ALL: Heil Hitler.

NIKOLAI: Heil yourself.

(OBERGRUPPENFUHRER GENERAL HEINRICH VON ASCELMEN is an imposing figure. In his 30-40s and dressed in his General's uniform he cuts a devastating figure of power. He's incensed and is about to slap NIKOLAI but holds back. He keeps his arm raised. He stares at NIKOLAI.)

GENERAL: *(To NIKOLAI.)* Heil Hitler.

(NIKOLAI looks away. The GENERAL lowers his arm. DOCTOR VÆRNET finds this very odd.)

GENERAL: *(Loud.)* Heil Hitler!!!

(NIKOLAI stands and eyeballs the GENERAL. He salutes.)

NIKOLAI: Heil Hitler.

(The GENERAL, smiles with satisfaction. NIKOLAI continues to glare at him. The GENERAL breaks and looks around to get his bearings, and goes over to DOCTOR VÆRNET. NIKOLAI sits. As the GENERAL addresses DOCTOR VÆRNET, FREDERICH fetches a small round side table. He places next to the chair. The GUARD exits to

fetch Champagne in an ice bucket and a crystal Champagne glass.
He pours. Throughout the scene the GENERAL sips champagne as
FREDERICH or the GUARD refills his glass.)

GENERAL: Doctor Værnet?

VÆRNET: You are most welcome Herr General.

GENERAL: Is this your surgery?

VÆRNET: Yes.

GENERAL: Not very impressive for a doctor with your
             reputation.

VÆRNET: Perhaps not but it's all mine, Herr General.

GENERAL: Should we become friends Herr Doctor you
             will call me Heinrich.

VÆRNET: The General does me too much honour.

GENERAL: I hear great things about your hormone
             therapy.

(The GENERAL wanders about sipping Champagne.)

VÆRNET: I've had great success in the past.

GENERAL: Yes so I gather, pity we haven't met before,
             perhaps you were able to cure my poor
             mother.

VÆRNET: I'm desolate to hear that.

GENERAL: In the end it was cancer that took her away.

VÆRNET: That therapy was not a cure as such, but it
             would've extended her life by quite a few years.

GENERAL: Enough for her to see me become
             Obergruppenfuhrer.

VÆRNET: Most certainly.

GENERAL: That makes it all the more distressing.

VÆRNET: Fate cannot be defeated.

GENERAL: There is no room for fate in the Third Reich
             Herr Doctor, we must abide by certain cast
             iron rules and leave nothing to chance.

VÆRNET: That is my most fervent wish, which is why I'm
             so deeply honoured you are interested in my
             new shortwave hormone therapy.

NIKOLAI: If you don't need me … *(He gets up to go.)*

GENERAL: *(Curt.)* One move and you'll be shot.
             (NIKOLAI sits.)

*(The GENERAL moves away. He puts his hand out and FREDERICH
re-fills his glass. He sips and stands next to ILSE.)*

GENERAL: Name.

ILSE: Ilse Paulsen Herr General.

GENERAL: Ilse? *(Excited.)* Are you named after Ilse Koch?

ILSE: No.

GENERAL: Ilse Koch is a great friend and asset to the
             Third Reich; in only a few months she has
             displaced over 30,000 Jews and undesirables.

ILSE: Displaced?

GENERAL: Moved them on.

ILSE: How?

GENERAL: Oh it's a most entertaining story. You see Ilse
             runs around the camp naked and anyone who
             looks at her is shot. It's a very effective method.
             (Beat.) One day I'll take you to see it if you
             like, it's quite a spectacle.

*(Silence. ILSE is shocked and doesn't know what to say. Her mouth
is dry, clears her throat and finds her resolve.)*

ILSE: I was named after my grandmother.

GENERAL: Is she still alive?

ILSE: No.

GENERAL: *(Smiles.)* Pity, she gave you a great name.

ILSE: Thank you.

GENERAL: How long have you been working for the good Doctor.

ILSE: Three years.

GENERAL: Three years, that's very good; so … um … you must know all about his therapies.

ILSE: Doctor Værnet has not taught me his latest discovery.

(The GENERAL turns to DOCTOR VÆRNET.)

GENERAL: Why not? *(He drinks.)*

VÆRNET: As I said it's new and only been tested a few times.

GENERAL: Don't you need your nurse to assist you?

VÆRNET: I work alone in the first instance. Ilse is only required in the final stages.

GENERAL: What an unusual method.

VÆRNET: One that has worked very well in the past.

(Suddenly the GENERAL turns back to ILSE.)

GENERAL: Are you married?

ILSE: *(Taken aback.)* No Herr General.

GENERAL: Is there a boy serenading you late into the night.

ILSE: There was a junior doctor and like all junior doctors they chase nurses. I let him catch me but the inevitable happened, he found another nurse. Dreams fade Herr General.

GENERAL: We all need dreams.

ILSE: These are not times to fall in love again.

GENERAL: But Denmark is part of the Third Reich, what better time to fall in love, to live one's life in the safe, secure world created by our Fuhrer.

ILSE: I don't have a beau Herr General.

GENERAL: *(Smiles.)* Well if you are ever in need of a man, I will make Frederich available.

ILSE: *(Shocked.)* But he's no more than a boy!!!

GENERAL: Yes but he's full of stamina. *(He laughs.)*

ILSE: *(Annoyed.)* I prefer to choose my own partners, thank you.

GENERAL: Maybe a sip of Champagne will help.

ILSE: I don't drink when I'm working.

GENERAL: Very wise … but it's never stopped me.

ILSE: You are a General; a nurse needs a clear head.

GENERAL: Feisty little thing, aren't you … *(He smiles.)*

(The GENERAL turns to NIKOLAI, looks at him but doesn't speak. VÆRNET feels awkward as fear sets in.)

GENERAL: *(To NIKOLAI.)* Why is he here?

VÆRNET: He's an undesirable Herr General, picked at random. He was walking the streets late at night.

GENERAL: An undesirable? Oh so that's what they look like. *(He lifts NIKOLAI's head.)* How cunning, they look perfectly normal.

VÆRNET: He's a homosexual.

NIKOLAI: Bastard!!!

(The GENERAL lifts his hand ever so slightly and FREDERICH punches NIKOLAI in the jaw. NIKOLAI is thrown off the chair and falls to the floor in agony. FREDERICH and the GUARD close in on NIKOLAI.)

GENERAL: Tell me.

VÆRNET:	Undesirables threaten the Third Reich, solutions must be found.
GENERAL:	I trust that is why I'm here today.
VÆRNET:	Absolutely.
GENERAL:	Good.

(DOCTOR VÆRNET goes to NIKOLAI.)

VÆRNET:	Take off your clothes.
NIKOLAI:	Get away from me.
VÆRNET:	*(Loud.)* Take them off.
NIKOLAI:	Never.

(DOCTOR VÆRNET looks at the GENERAL. The GENERAL nods and FREDERICH fires a warning shot. ILSE lets out a cry. The shot is deafening. NIKOLAI realises they are not playing games and starts to take off his clothes. He strips down to his underpants.)

VÆRNET:	I have developed a hormone therapy that can convert sexual orientation.
GENERAL:	Does SS-Reichsfuhrer Himmler know about this?
VÆRNET:	Not yet.
GENERAL:	*(Excited.)* Oh good, if successful may I tell him, *(Pleads.)* please?
VÆRNET:	Oh General the honour will be mine. *(Bows slightly.)* You see, a man like any other.
GENERAL:	Incredible.
VÆRNET:	Put him on the bed.
NIKOLAI:	*(Trying to escape.)* No, what are you …

(FREDERICH punches him in the stomach and winds him. NIKOLAI keels over. FREDERICH and the GUARD grab him and force him onto the table. Together with ILSE they strap him down. Throughout, NIKOLAI tries to resist with ….)

NIKOLAI: No … let me go … leave me … get away from me … let go …

(He struggles, fighting as hard as he can but is overpowered. Finally he is strapped down. ILSE moves the screen in order to shield NIKOLAI'S modesty. The GENERAL is annoyed his glass is empty; he raises it into the air. FREDERICH panics.)

FREDERICH: Forgive me, Herr General.

(FREDERICH swiftly fills the GENERAL's glass. DOCTOR VÆRNET goes to NIKOLAI.)

VÆRNET: There is nothing to be afraid of; I'm going to help you get better.

NIKOLAI: Animal.

VÆRNET: You'll have a much happier life.

NIKOLAI: Pig.

GENERAL: This could be such an admirable solution Herr Doctor; it removes the necessity to throw them into labour camps, thus freeing space for Jews.

VÆRNET: My thought exactly.

GENERAL: We have such a problem of storage, our forces are so efficient they keep finding Jews and filling up our camps. *(He sips.)* If only Australia was not part of the British Empire we could send them all there, oh well.

VÆRNET: When Britain falls, we'll follow your advice.

GENERAL: Pity you don't have a therapy to combat the Jewish faith.

NIKOLAI: You can't do that!!!

(DOCTOR VÆRNET turns on NIKOLAI.)

VÆRNET: Gag him.

NIKOLAI: No, what are you going to do?

(FREDERICH and the GUARD gag NIKOLAI with a metal rod and tie his head down.)

VÆRNET: *(To ILSE.)* Is everything ready?

ILSE: Yes.

VÆRNET: Remove his pants.

(Only NIKOLAI's head and shoulders are visible. He struggles to break free but the gag muffles his ugly sounds. The GENERAL goes to his chair and sits. He gulps down the Champagne and puts his hand out. FREDERICH pours him more Champagne.)

GENERAL: This is very good Champagne, where did you get it.

FREDERICH: The SS allowed us access to their cellar, especially for Herr General.

GENRAL: Ahhh how very kind. Frederich joined us in Czechoslovakia and has been invaluable ever since. You should apply for an assistant Herr Doctor, you won't regret it.

VÆRNET: This is not the appropriate time.

GENERAL: As you wish.

VÆRNET: *(Caresses NIKOLAI's head.)* Dear boy, don't be frightened, all you'll feel is a little scratch.

(DOCTOR VÆRNET picks up a large syringe and a phial. He inserts the needle into the phial and extracts a tiny capsule.

NIKOLAI becomes ever more agitated, he tries to speak, but can only muster sounds of fear. His eyes express his agony.)

VÆRNET: This, Herr General, is an artificial gland in the form of a tiny capsule made from the male hormone testosterone of a monkey …

GENERAL: *(Laughs.)* Monkeys?

ILSE: You killed a monkey for your …

VÆRNET: It was already dead. The Danish Institute of Health and Research kindly donated a monkey from which I extracted the testosterone and created a formula to be reproduced artificially.

GENERAL: Go on.

VÆRNET: Once injected it'll remove all homosexual thoughts and desires.

GENERAL: Well done.

VÆRNET: The capsule ejects tiny molecules that once absorbed into the system the patient will dream of women.

GENERAL: Naturally.

VÆRNET: It's a new vaccine.

GENERAL: Interesting.

VÆRNET: And it's very cheap to produce.

GENERAL: How cheap?

VÆRNET: A mere twenty Reichfenning.

GENERAL: Excellent.

(NIKOLAI screams are muffled but the fear is sickening.)

GENERAL: Carry on your good work Doctor, all these ugly sounds bore me.

VÆRNET: Very well … *(To NIKOLAI.)* You must be brave; don't you want to be cured?

(DOCTOR VÆRNET nears NIKOLAI's groin. NIKOLAI terror has no bounds.)

VÆRNET: To have maximum effect it must be injected into both testicles.

(The GENERAL is horrified, he downs his drink. As DOCTOR VÆRNET is about to inject NIKOLAI …

BLACK OUT.

NIKOLAI's scream shudders through the darkness. They exit.)

***   ***   ***

OBERGRUPPENFUHRER GENERAL VON AESCHELMAN remains seated next to his Champagne. A single dim light shines over him. He drinks and his smug expression reveals his delight. Jazz music starts to play faintly in the background. The GENERAL stands and starts to remove his jacket and necktie. He looks more relaxed as his General persona fades. He drinks. FREDERICH and the GUARD enter and re-dress the set as if it's a lush boudoir. They cover the bed with a velvet throw and large ornate cushions. The GENERAL sways to the music. FREDERICH checks the Champagne and brings a fresh bottle and another glass. The GENERAL is lost in his world. The GUARD exits and returns with a box. He places it on the table. The scene is dimly lit as if in a cabaret club. FREDERICH and the GUARD exit quietly without saluting. The GENERAL pours himself another glass and drinks. He hums to himself. GEORG enters.

He's almost naked under his long dressing gown and is bare foot. He stands by the door observing the GENERAL, who doesn't see him.

GEORG: Had a difficult day?

GENERAL: Not especially.

GEORG: Drinking already?

GENERAL: *(Smiles.)* I've been doing that since this morning.

GEORG: One might say you're an alcoholic.

GENERAL: Champagne doesn't count as alcohol.

GEORG: Really, never knew that.

GENERAL: Would you like a drop?

GEORG: Not yet.

GENERAL: Need to work up a thirst?

GEORG: Something like that.

(The GENERAL drinks, he's starting to be unsteady on his feet.)

GENERAL: What did you do today?

GEORG: Waited.

GENERAL: *(Laughs.)* For me?

GEORG: Of course.

GENERAL: Did you dream up a game?

GEORG: No.

GENERAL: Pity, I'm in the mood to play.

GEORG: Let's play then.

  (The GENERAL moves away.)

GENERAL: Did I ever tell you I hate blond people?

GEORG: No.

GENERAL: I do, they look insipid, vacant like a white rat.

GEORG: and Aryan

GENERAL: Hate them.

GEORG: Interesting.

  (Pause. The GENERAL stares at GEORG.)

GENERAL: Take that … *(He gestures.)* that … that gown off.

GEORG: I'll catch cold.

GENERAL: *(Shouts.)* Take it off.

GEORG: You better stop drinking.

GENERAL: What are you doing here?

GEORG: Shouldn't I be asking that; after all I was
              arrested for no reason, stripped naked, kept
              in a luxurious bedroom so you can watch me,
              touch me …

GENERAL: Oh so I did …

  (The GENERAL looks at GEORG full of lust yet full of guilt.)

GENERAL: *(Softly.)* I want to see you naked.

GEORG: Why?

GENERAL: Because I want to …

GEORG: You're like a spoilt child.

GENERAL: *(Shouts.)* Do as I say.

GEORG: *(Quietly.)* You can't see me when you're drunk. *(Pause.)* I'll come back when you're more reasonable.

(GEORG turns to leave.)

GENERAL: Where are you going, get back here …

GEORG: I didn't know what was going to become of me. I was bundled into a truck along with a group of men the night my club closed. You had all the power but the moment you turned me into your 'plaything' you lost everything. Isn't it funny that in just a few days I know everything about you? *(Beat.)* I'm leaving.

GENERAL: You have NOTHING on me!!! No one will believe you.

GEORG: Rumours always begin with the truth.

(GEORG heads out.)

GENERAL: *(Loud.)* Get back here at once or I'll have you shot.

GEORG: Oh really? And how are you going to explain the presence of a half-naked dead man in your quarters.

(Silence.)

GENERAL: *(Softens.)* I want you.

GEORG: I know.

GENERAL: Please, forgive me … come here.

GEORG: All bravado and yet such a baby.

GENERAL: Hold me …

(GEORG looks at him, relents and then goes over to him.)

GEORG: I should scold you …

GENERAL: I need you.

GEORG: A man in constant need.

GENERAL: *(Pleads.)* Please …

GEORG: Begging doesn't suit an Obergruppenfuhrer.

GENERAL: I'm not that when I'm with you.

GEORG: What are you then?

GENERAL: A man, just a man.

(The GENERAL takes hold of GEORG and holds him tight. He rubs his hands up his back and pulls him close and then kisses him.)

GENERAL: Don't go …

GEORG: You're trembling.

(GEORG pulls away.)

GENERAL: You're not the only one, you know?

GEORG: I'm aware of that.

GENERAL: I can pick and choose.

GEORG: Most put up a fight, I'm more willing.

GENERAL: It's not that, never that. You're aloof, difficult to catch, always teasing, playing games. Your retorts are quick, snappy. I have to have my wits about me; you're mysterious, intriguing, and special. *(Beat.)* You make me feel alive in a world so full of horror. I've never felt like this, it's exciting.

GEORG: Too much excitement can go to your head.

GENERAL: I want to decorate you.

GEORG: I'm not a Christmas tree.

GENERAL: I want to see you sparkle.

GEORG: Like tinsel.

GENERAL: Nothing as cheap as that.

(He loosens his grip and goes to the table and opens the box. He pulls out a hand full of jewels and goes to GEORG.)

GENERAL: Choose what you like.

GEORG: To what end?

GENERAL: Your cabaret act is famous. I've never seen it. I want you dressed in jewels; let's see if they suit you.

GEORG: And perform for you?

GENERAL: No, no need.

GEORG: Where do these trinkets come from?

GENERAL: Gathered from those who were moved on and no longer needed them.

(GEORG is shocked.)

GEORG: If I fail your expectations will you send the freak away for experimentation?

GENERAL: Not you, never you.

(GEORG moves away and starts to put on some of the jewellery; a bracelet, a string of pearls and a diamond necklace. He looks ridiculous but the GENERAL is in awe. The GENERAL goes to him.)

GENERAL: Stay with me.

GEORG: What's happened?

GENERAL: It's this world …

GEORG: Do you want to stop?

GENERAL: It's suffocating me.

GEORG: You know you can't.

GENERAL: Yes, that's it, yes … *(Defeated.)* I know.

GEORG: Why?

GENERAL: Be with me.

GEORG: I have to.

GENERAL: No you must want to.

GEORG: *(Faint smile.)* Never that!

(The GENERAL kisses him again.)

GEORG: Champagne bubbles have a strange effect on people.

GENERAL: Never jest about the truth.

(Suddenly GEORG realises his power. He moves away, leaving the GENERAL aching in his love/lust.)

GEORG: Your emotions have betrayed your rank.

GENERAL: My feelings are true.

GEORG: How sweet lust is when it's about to destroy you.

GENERAL: Only you can do that.

GEORG: How feeble men are. When in a heightened state you're all the same.

GENERAL: End my misery.

GEORG: Release the pressure.

GENERAL: How?

GEORG: It's in your hands.

GENERAL: You don't understand.

GEORG: Oh but I do.

GENERAL: You have no idea what it's like having nothing, knowing your entire country has been

humiliated, made to feel like the pariah of
the world because of the Kaiser's ego. There
was no choice but to follow the road of hope
and self-esteem. It was only Adolph Hitler
that makes us feel whole again, respected.
Germany is a force once more, strong, healthy,
the mixture is intoxicating. We rallied around
him, cheered him on; attended his vast rallies,
proud to be German again. *(Pause.)* And yet I
never expected how claustrophobic his regime
is; if you put your little finger out of place that
you're somehow a traitor to the cause. *(Beat.)*
Your life is taken away from you; you are no
longer a person merely a number, a cog in this
great machine that is the Third Reich. *(Beat.)*
I don't know who I am anymore?

GEORG: You are an Obergruppenfuhrer …

GENERAL: What is that?

GEORG: A brilliant General that has used every
           opportunity to reach such glorious heights at
           such a young age.

GENERAL: You talk of glory.

GEORG: For the glory of your nation.

GENERAL: It may be glorious to die for your country on a
           battlefield but it means nothing if you're a man
           on fire and yet, still breathing.

(GEORG doesn't feel sorry but pities his predicament.)

GEORG: If I stay will it help?

GENERAL: Only until I awake.

GEORG: Then we'll sleep all night …

GENERAL: and in the morning I'll need to gather myself,
           put on my uniform and face the day with
           another performance to match yesterday's
           farce.

(GEORG goes to him and kisses him tenderly on the cheek.)

GEORG: The whole night has to pass before dawn.

GENERAL: At which point I'll meet my Waterloo.

GEORG: There is time for that.

(GEORG smiles and takes the GENERAL's hand and guides him out as ZACK TRAVIS enters and watches them leave as the lights change.)

***   ***   ***

DOCTOR CARL PETER VÆRNET'S SURGERY.

It's a bright sunny day. ZACK looks around; he's agitated, worried. DOCTOR VÆRNET enters. He's full of self-importance and excited by the prospect of a new patient.

VÆRNET: Good Morning, I'm Doctor Carl Værnet?

(He extends his hand. ZACK doesn't shake it.)

ZACK: I'm not a patient.

VÆRNET: *(Taken aback.)* Would you like to register with my nurse.

ZACK: No.

VÆRNET: I'm open to take on new patients, please don't be shy.

ZACK: I'm not in need of medical assistance.

VÆRNET: Oh, is there anything else I can help …

ZACK: Yes, I'm looking for someone.

VÆRNET: I'm a General Practitioner; I don't deal in missing persons.

ZACK: Yes, but he was brought here, to see you.

VÆRNET: *(Suspicious.)* Here?

ZACK: There is always a network of resistance and spies when countries are at war. People are watched, even doctors. I know he was brought here.

VÆRNET: You Americans think you know everything! You know nothing!!!

ZACK: Why are you hiding him?

VÆRNET: I'm not hiding anyone.

ZACK: My information comes from the Danish authorities.

VÆRNET: Who are under the orders of the Third Reich!

ZACK: Denmark has retained its autonomy over its judicial system; it was not difficult finding out what happened to its citizens.

VÆRNET: Then if you know everything, why are you asking me?

ZACK: Because he disappeared. Where is he?

VÆRNET: Who?

ZACK: Nikolai Bergsen.

(DOCTOR VÆRNET stiffens and changes tone.)

VÆRNET: I don't know that name.

ZACK: I say you do.

VÆRNET: Nonsense.

ZACK: Do you know what's happened to him?

VÆRNET: I don't know what you are talking about? Now please, I'm very busy I'm already late for my rounds.

(He heads out.)

ZACK: You won't say, will you?

VÆRNET: Nurse Ilse will show you out.

ZACK: How can a doctor go on his rounds without his bag?

(DOCTOR VÆRNET stops.)

VÆRNET: My day bag is always ready by the front door.

ZACK: I didn't see it.

VÆRNET: I must ask you to leave, please.

ZACK: You should practise your lying skills Doctor, they stink.

VÆRNET: If you don't leave I shall call the authorities.

ZACK: I was arrested the same night as Nikolai Bergsen only difference he's nowhere to be found.

(DOCTOR VÆRNET glares at ZACK.)

VÆRNET: There is nothing for you here.

(As DOCTOR VÆRNET leaves.)

VÆRNET: Good day to you.   *(He's gone.)*

(ZACK is left in no doubt that NIKOLAI was there, he starts to look around to see if he can find any evidence but it's all so pristine and clinical that there is nothing. ILSE enters, ZACK doesn't see her. She looks at him. Pause.)

ILSE: Why are you looking for him? Is he family?

(ZACK turns.)

ZACK: Ah … no … He's ah, … ah … a friend.

ILSE: *(Saddened.)* I see.

ZACK: Did you see him?

ILSE: Briefly.

ZACK: So he was here!

ILSE: Please leave, I don't want to get into trouble.

ZACK: I won't tell anyone, I swear, but please tell me, where is he?

ILSE: I … I don't know.

ZACK: What is the matter with you people, why won't you tell the truth?

ILSE: It's difficult for me, I live on my own; if I don't work there is no one to help me. I can't afford to lose my job.

ZACK: You don't understand, they're scaling back the Embassy staff. I'm going back to America;

I can't leave not knowing what's happened to him.

ILSE: Nothing happened. He was arrested.

ZACK: Please, I'll be on the other side of the world worrying about him, tell me.

ILSE: When certain people are arrested they are seen by a doctor …

ZACK: Why, for what?

ILSE: To judge the best place to put them.

ZACK: But Nikolai is strong and healthy …

ILSE: Yes, that's it … that's why he was seen so quickly.

ZACK: And then where did they take him?

ILSE: Away.

ZACK: Away, where?

ILSE: I don't know.

(ZACK is getting very angry, gets close to her, menacing.)

ZACK: I'm not known to be a violent man but if you don't tell me I'll smash this place up.

ILSE: He's been held by the Frikorps Danmark.

ZACK: Why?

ILSE: For further interrogation

ZACK: He works in an art gallery for Christ's sake, he's not a criminal.

ILSE: *(Lies.)* I … I believe they are investigating the gallery.

ZACK: The gallery has a clean record, why are they investigating it.

ILSE: It has something to do with a forged painting.

ZACK: What painting?

ILSE: A Chagall, I believe.

ZACK: Why would they question Nikolai about a
               forged Chagall in a doctor's surgery?

(ILSE is getting deeper into trouble as the lies mount up.)

ILSE: They checked his medical condition and then
               asked about his work, the gallery and the
               painting. *(Irritated.)* People talk.

ZACK: People don't talk about a painting with a
               Doctor.

ILSE: It wasn't the Doctor, it was the Frikorps …

ZACK: *(Incredulous.)* Do you know who I should talk
               to?

ILSE: What business do I have with the Frikorps?

ZACK: *(Calmer.)* Is he in prison?

ILSE: Yes.

(ZACK moves, not knowing what to do, lost.)

ZACK: If only I had a few days, I could get the
               Embassy to arrange a meeting with the
               Frikorps, talk to them …

ILSE: That'll be of no use.

ZACK: I'm shipped out in few hours. *(Angry.)* I have to
               know if he's okay … what they've done to him
               …

(ILSE walks away, she feels desperately guilty.)

ILSE: It's all the more tragic when you're …

ZACK: Sure is …

*(ZACK feels desponded and defeated. He moves away. ILSE looks at
him full of pity.)*

ILSE: I'll try to help.

ZACK:	How?
ILSE:	If I see him, maybe I can call you; give you some news, if you give me a phone number.
ZACK:	*(Excited.)* You get to see the inmates?
ILSE:	Sometimes they ask me to take blood, to test prisoners for diseases …
ZACK:	But they'll search you and find it.
ILSE:	It's not difficult to hide a number.
ZACK:	But
ILSE:	Maybe you don't want to …
ZACK:	No, of course I'll give it to you, it's just you may lose it.

(ZACK is very agitated.)

ILSE:	I'll keep a copy, just in case.
ZACK:	But that's putting you in danger.
ILSE:	Love is nothing without risks.

(ZACK takes out a business card. It's seems quite worn and hands it to ILSE.)

ZACK:	That is my parent's home in Connecticut; it's the safest place to call.
ILSE:	It's tatty.
ZACK:	It's been in my wallet since I left home for Harvard.
ILSE:	I see.
ZACK:	*(Ever more desperate.)* Please find him …
ILSE:	I'll try.
ZACK:	If you see him, tell him I will come back and take him away, please.

ILSE: Of course.

(ZACK paces about full of stress and anguish.)

ZACK: We did nothing wrong, Christ what a mess.
               (To himself.) I'll stay, that's what I'll do, I'll
               take my chances and stay in Copenhagen
               … but they'll arrest me … yes … I have no
               choice I must go back to America. *(Screams in
               frustration!.)* FUCK!!! *(He moves away then turns
               to ILSE with steely determination.)* I will find him,
               I will take him away; we will be together.

*(ILSE knows NIKOLAI will never be the same, her heart is breaking
but there is nothing she can do. Her eyes are full of emotion.)*

ILSE: I hope one day I'll be loved as much …

ZACK: Call me!!! *(Softer.)* Please.

ILSE: I promise …

(ZACK watches ILSE put the card away as the lights fade ….)

***   ***   ***

*DOCTOR CARL PETER VÆRNET's SURGERY. A few days later. Once
again ILSE is placing the instruments on a chrome platter, placing the
sheet over the bed and preparing the surgery for the day. DOCTOR CARL
PETER VÆRNET enters. He's excited and in a very good mood.*

VÆRNET: Herr General is on his way.

ILSE: So you keep saying.

VÆRNET: Have I?

ILSE: About ten times.

VÆRNET: What time is it?

ILSE: Eleven.

VÆRNET: He's late.

ILSE: No he's not.

VÆRNET: What's the matter with you this morning, are you not excited?

ILSE: I'm doing my job.

VÆRNET: What's come over you lately, you're always so sullen.

ILSE: We live in sad times.

VÆRNET: Nonsense, what greater joy than to belong to a world that is clean and pure.

LISE: It can only be pure without human kind.

VÆRNET: What do you think I'm trying doing?

ILSE: Indeed.

VÆRNET: Well I'm not going to spoil the greatest day of my life but listening to a misery like you.

ILSE: I'm just laying out your instruments; that's all.

VÆRNET: What time is it?

ILSE: Time you bought a watch.

VÆRNET: Huh!!!

(ILSE smiles and continues her work as DOCTOR VÆRNET paces about. FREDERICH enters without warning and full of arrogance.)

FREDERICH: Where do you want him?

VÆRNET: Not sure, where is the General?

FREDERICH: On his way up.

VÆRNET: Then we'll wait for him.

FREDERICH: Yes, Herr Doctor. *(He stands to one side at attention.)*

ILSE: *(Watching him.)* Are you always so fierce or do you smile sometimes?

VÆRNET: Be quiet.

ILSE: He looks like a Roman statue.

VÆRNET: Keep your comments to yourself, you stupid girl.

(ILSE laughs quietly to herself. OBERGRUPPENFUHRER GENERAL HEINRICH VON AESCHELMAN enters followed by his GUARD.)

ALL: Heil Hitler.

GENERAL: Forgive me Herr Doctor but breakfast was long and there was a problem with the car, they couldn't find it or something, simply ridiculous.

VÆRNET: Think nothing of it Herr General.

GENERAL: Well, what have you got for me?

VÆRNET: A most exciting day, most exciting.

(DOCTOR VÆRNET gestures to FREDERICH who leaves immediately followed by the GUARD.)

GENERAL: *(To ILSE.)* You'll wear them out, if you keep rubbing them like that.

ILSE: All instruments must be sterilized.

GENERAL: Don't see the point myself; they'll be moved on quicker if they get an infection.

VÆRNET: The General's methods are most admirable.

(They wait in silence. The GENERAL is getting impatient, bored.)

GENERAL: Will this take long?

VÆRNET: We should savour such an auspicious day, Herr General.

GENERAL: Ummm …

(FREDERICH enters with NIKOLAI. NIKOLAI spirit has been broken. NIKOLAI has a vacant distant expression, one of a man that has been defeated and humiliated. His clothes are torn and filthy. He's somewhat unsteady on his feet but refuses and help. FREDERICH stands next to him. The GENERAL is the first to see him.)

GENERAL:	Oh no, not this one again, Herr Doctor I didn't come here …
VÆRNET:	If the General will indulge me for a moment. *(He bows slightly.)*
GENERAL:	Oh very well.
VÆRNET:	Too kind. *(Turn to FREDERICH.)* Sit him over there.

(FREDERICH grabs his arm and dumps him on a chair. NIKOLAI sits slumped on the chair and looks away. He's dressed in a pair of cotton trousers and a shirt. He's barefoot.)

| VÆRNET: | *(To the GENERAL.)* May I? |

(The GENERAL waves his hand in approval.)

VÆRNET:	Thank you. Today I'm going to prove to you, that my cure of homosexuality …
GENERAL:	Oh that word again, it sticks in my throat.
VÆRNET:	That my cure is the only one in the world that is successful.
GENERAL:	*(Surprised, shocked.)* There are others?
VÆRNET:	All quacks, Herr General, not like me.
GENERAL:	*(Worried.)* Where?
VÆRNET:	America, Africa nothing for you to worry about as Europe will be clean soon.
GENERAL:	*(Turns away.)* Quite.

(DOCTOR VÆRNET turns to NIKOLAI.)

| VÆRNET: | Stand up. |

(NIKOLAI doesn't move.)

| VÆRNET: | *(Loud.)* Stand up! |

(NIKOLAI stands awkwardly.)

| VÆRNET: | Remove your trousers. |

NIKOLAI: No.

VÆRNET: *(Slaps him hard. Loud.)* Take them off!!!

(NIKOLAI winces in pain and slowly drops his trousers. His underpants have been removed and his torn, tatty shirt hangs low.)

VÆRNET: Step out of them.

(NIKOLAI steps away from his trousers.)

VÆRNET: Remove your shirt.

NIKOLAI: *(Embarrassed, humiliated.)* No!

(FREDERICH draws his gun and points it at NIKOLAI. NIKOLAI and FREDERICH eyeball each other; NIKOLAI relents and removes his shirt and stands naked. He holds his hands over his groin.)

VÆRNET: Stand over there with your back to us.

NIKOLAI: Why?

VÆRNET: *(Shouts.)* Over there. *(NIKOLAI stands in the corner with his back turned.)* May I have the General's kind permission to address your guard?

GENERAL: *(Waving his hand.)* Be my guest.

VÆRNET: *(Bows.)* Thank you; much obliged. *(To FREDERICH.)* You can fetch the other convict.

(FREDERICH clicks his heels and exits. The GENERAL is getting irritated and nervous. Moments later FREDERICH enters with GEORG. The GENERAL is shocked.

GEORG is bare-chested and wears a pair of linen or fine sack cloth trousers loosely fitted around his waist and is barefoot. FREDERICH holds his arm. NIKOLAI doesn't move.)

GENERAL: *(His throat is dry.)* What are … why is he here?

VÆRNET: At my request, Herr General.

GENERAL: *(Agitated.)* What for?

VÆRNET: I need a healthy convict, one that didn't look ill.

GENERAL: There are many others that …

VÆRNET: But he's here now, what difference does it make?

GENERAL: *(Very uneasy.)* Yes … well …

VÆRNET: Thank you.

(Naturally GEORG recognises the GENERAL but doesn't let on; instead he stands looking straight ahead refusing to make eye contact with the GENERAL. ILSE notices and understands what's going on whereas DOCTOR VÆRNET is oblivious to the situation.)

ILSE: Know this man Herr General?

GENERAL: No, what makes you say that?

ILSE: *(Smiles.)* Oh, nothing.

VÆRNET: Do your work.

ILSE: Yes, Doctor.

VÆRNET: *(To GEORG.)* Come over here … *(GEORG doesn't move. DOCTOR VÆRNET looks at the GENERAL.)*

GENERAL: Do as the Doctor says, please.

VÆRNET: *(Shocked.)* PLEASE!!! *(Loud, determined.)* get over here.

(FREDERICH lets go of GEORG and he walks towards the DOCTOR.)

GEORG: Do you know the colour of blood?

VÆRNET: *(Taken aback.)* What?

GEORG: Do you know the colour of blood?

VÆRNET: Red, everyone knows it's red.

GEORG: No, it's purple; it only turns red when it's mixed with oxygen.

(DOCTOR VÆRNET is caught out, embarrassed. He becomes edgy and agitated.)

VÆRNET: Such impertinence; *(Loud.)* Remove your
                 trousers …

GEORG: What? No.

VÆRNET: Ilse prepare the bed.

GEORG: NO!

VÆRNET: *(Forcibly.)* Remove your trousers.

(GEORG removes his trousers; his underpants have also been removed. He stands naked with his hands covering his groin. DOCTOR VÆRNET is happy with the scene.)

VÆRNET: *(Smiles.)* Very good. Hands on your sides both
                 of you. *(They don't obey.)* NOW!

(NIKOLAI and GEORG drop their hands. Both are naked and exposed.)

VÆRNET: *(With great excitement and trepidation.*
                 To NIKOLAI.) Turn around. *(Nothing.)*
                 TURN around …

(NIKOLAI turns around and is shocked to see GEORG standing naked in front of him.)

GEORG: *(To NIKOLAI.)* Don't move

VÆRNET: Quiet.

GEORG: Look at me …

VÆRNET: Shut up!

GEORG: Think of nothing.

VÆRNET: *(Shouts.)* SILENCE!!!

(Tears drop down NIKOLAI's face as he watches GEORG's face with an expression of pure love and solidarity.)

NIKOLAI: A rose is still a rose.

(GEORG manages a faint smile. The GENERAL looks away not able to watch such savage humiliation. Neither man is aroused in

the slightest. *DOCTOR VÆRNET is only interested in NIKOLAI and is beyond excitement.)*

VÆRNET: Don't move; we must wait …

(NIKOLAI and GEORG stare at each other without moving a muscle. The GENERAL is very uncomfortable. ILSE holds a handkerchief to her mouth. The torture seems to go on for hours.

DOCTOR VÆRNET watches NIKOLAI intently, quietly praying that he will not get aroused. With all that NIKOLAI has gone through there is no chance that he would. As the minutes pass DOCTOR VÆRNET becomes agitated with excitement. At last DOCTOR VÆRNET announces his triumph, arms stretched out like a Roman Emperor.)

VÆRNET: Standing before you is my greatest achievement and triumph. This Herr General; is concrete proof that my hormone therapy works. I paraded a naked man in front of this unfortunate individual and as you can see he is NOT aroused in the slightest. Several days have passed and the molecules have dissolved releasing the male hormones into his blood removing any unclean urges and thoughts. *(Beat.)* I declare before witnesses here present, that I Doctor Carl Peter Værnet have successfully found the correct formula and consequently the CURE for homosexuality. *(He bows.)*

(There is no applause instead the room is silent in shock. The GENERAL breaks the silence with a muted applause. ILSE and FREDERICH don't applaud. DOCTOR VÆRNET is beyond delighted and beams like a peacock.)

GENERAL: Bravo, bravo …

VÆRNET: Thank you, thank you …

GENERAL: I must admit, I doubted you at first … but you proved me wrong.

VÆRNET: I was never in any doubt.

GENERAL: Well done, Herr Doctor, well done …

(DOCTOR VÆRNET is beaming with pride. GEORG and NIKOLAI keep looking at each other and don't move. The GENERAL feels awkward. He addresses his guards.)

GENERAL: Take them away.

FREDERICH: Yes, Herr General.

(GEORG and NIKOLAI pick up their clothes and hold him in front to cover their modesty. FREDERICH grabs GEORG's arm and shoves him out. DOCTOR VÆRNET shoves NIKOLAI out. They exit.)

GENERAL: Tell me Doctor, will the prisoner be able to function as normal … you know … with a woman?

VÆRNET: Certainly, he will be as normal as you and I.

GENERAL: Ah yes … remarkable.

VÆRNET: My cure is fast, cheap and effective. It can be applied to thousands of sick men offering them a safe cure and freedom from that destructive disease.

GENERAL: *(Gets up and goes to shake the Doctor's hand.)* Congratulations, Herr Doctor, congratulations …

VÆRNET: You're too kind Herr General … too kind.

GENERAL: Call me Heinrich …

VÆRNET: The honour is all mine … ah … Heinrich.

(The GENERAL gets up and paces about.)

GENERAL: I want to transfer you and your family to Prague as soon as possible.

VÆRNET: Prague?

GENERAL: Yes, we have a selection of grand apartments for you to choose from, they were all owned by Jews but they have moved on and left them vacant, I'm sure you and your family will be very comfortable there.

VÆRNET: We had never thought of leaving Copenhagen.

GENERAL: I will send my men to help you pack and transport all your belongings to Prague. I will make sure your move will be as painless as possible.

VÆRNET: Yes, but why Prague?

GENERAL: Prague is a very beautiful city.

VÆRNET: Indeed it is, I went there as boy.

GENERAL: You need to set up a medical facility there. Once that's established you'll move to Buchenwald, the labour camp with the largest number of homosexuals.

VÆRNET: I understand. *(Smiles.)*

GENERAL: Your family will travel first and you will accompany me to Berlin.

VÆRNET: *(Besides himself.)* Berlin?

GENERAL: You will present your credentials to Reichsfuhrer Himmler.

VAERNT: Himmler? Oh General that's too much.

GENERAL: Reichsfuhrer Himmler will put you under direct orders of SS Doctor Gerhard Schiedlausky.

VÆRNET: Does the Doctor deal in treatments?

GENERAL: He is experimenting on twins. He removes their organs, thus giving us a better understanding on why twins exist.

VÆRNET: Are his subjects dead?

GENERAL: Oh no, no, quite alive, there would be no point if they were dead.

VÆRNET: How very interesting.

GENERAL: You will need to leave at once.

ILSE: What is to become of the prisoner?

GENERAL: *(Turns to her.)* Did you not see? He's cured and
                 free to go.

ILSE: What about his papers?

GENERAL: Oh he'll be given all the necessary
                 documentation.

ILSE: Where will he go?

GENERAL: Wherever he likes, home, the Opera, the fun
                 fair …

(ILSE is taken aback. DOCTOR VÆRNET laughs.)

ILSE: And the other one?

GENERAL: *(Taken aback, doesn't quite know what to say.)*
                 He'll … he'll go back to …

ILSE: I see.

VÆRNET: I'm deeply honoured; I cannot wait to heal all
                 these unfortunate people.

GENERAL: Your job is to clear as much space for Jews as
                 possible.

VÆRNET: Of Course …

ILSE: What about my place?

GENERAL: You have assisted the good Doctor admirably
                 …

VÆRNET: My treatment would not be successful without
                 the help of my trusted nurse.

GENERAL: Of course. We will find a new post for her.

ILSE: I will only work in the hospital.

GENERAL: *(Smiles.)* Who am I to argue with such a
                 beautiful face?

ILSE: Thank you.

GENERAL: I would invite you all for a Champagne celebration but there is much work to be done …

VÆRNET: There certainly is …

(The GENERAL heads for the door. DOCTOR VÆRNET escorts him out.)

GERERAL: *(To ILSE.)* Good work …

ILSE: *(Quietly.)* Thank you.

VÆRNET: Allow me to show you to your car Herr General …

(As they leave …)

GENERAL: Heinrich, please …

VÆRNET: Of course … Heinrich …

(They exit. ILSE is left alone. She looks around. She can't believe what's just happened. She returns to her tray of instruments, she's in a daze, not knowing which way to turn. She picks up a syringe, holds it up and with quiet anger ….)

ILSE: Bastard!!!

(After a moment, she exits. Out of the darkness NIKOLAI enters. He's dressed in his light trousers, tatty shirt and broken worn boots. The stage darkens as he wanders into a weak light. He looks around. He has a vacant expression. He stops. His speech is garbled, jumbled at first but soon becomes coherent.)

NIKOLAI: *(Sings in a cracked voice.)* Underneath the lantern by the barrack gate … Twas there that you whispered … Time would come for us to part … orders came for sailing over there … *(He walks away out of the light.)* He'll come back … *(Beat.)* Where am I? Home is no more … there are strange people living there; I'm scared to go in. I'm not sure, is it still home? *(Beat.)* The gallery is closed. I'll wait here, maybe tomorrow it'll open; I can stay in the storeroom. Jansen won't mind. *(Beat.)* I'm cold, *(Beat.)* Christ I stink … I'm lost.

(Sings.) When we are marching in the mud and cold … *(Stops signing.)* I need a corner with no wind … drafts … yes the Corner Light Club … Georg … I don't know … I did nothing … *(Tears stream down his face.)* I did nothing wrong …

(ILSE enters and approaches tentatively.)

ILSE: Let me take you home.

(NIKOLAI takes fright.)

NIKOLAI: No, get away from me …

ILSE: I want to help you …

NIKOLAI: You were there, you helped him.

ILSE: I'll take care of you …

NIKOLAI: NO!!! You'll inject me …

ILSE: No, I won't …

NIKOLAI: Get away from me …

ILSE: Please …

NIKOLAI: I'll scream …

ILSE: Zack asked me to help you.

NIKOLAI: Zack?

ILSE: Yes.

NIKOLAI: Where is he?

ILSE: He's gone back …

NIKOLAI: Back?

ILSE: Come with me, I'll take you home …

NIKOLAI: Back home.

ILSE: You can have a bath and I'll prepare a broth, you can stay with me …

NIKOLAI: You, needles …

ILSE: No, needles, just me …

NIKOLAI: Zack?

ILSE: He will find you …

NIKOLAI: Yes … yes he said that …

ILSE: Come with me, its cold out here …

NIKOLAI: Needles …

ILSE: There are no more needles, I promise.

NIKOLAI: Promise …

ILSE: Yes … yes … just my home …

NIKOLAI: Home.

(ILSE takes NIKOLAI by the arm and they walk away as the lights change into a welcoming warm colour.

NIKOLAI sits on a chair as ILSE covers the bed with a throw and colourful cushions. On a small side table there is a radio that obscures a telephone. She switches on the radio and soft Classical music plays. NIKOLAI looks over then away again, distant, vacant. ILSE keeps an eye on him.)

ILSE: Would you like some tea?

NIKOLAI: *(Only half listening.)* What?

ILSE: Tea?

NIKOLAI: If you like.

ILSE: I won't be long.

NIKOLAI: Yes.

(ILSE exits. NIKOLAI remains seated, staring at the floor. He starts to feel secure and looks around. He doesn't see doctors or instruments instead a warm cosy home. He feels more comfortable. The music and stillness is comforting. He gets up and looks around feeling lost. ILSE enters with tea on a tray. She smiles.)

ILSE: *(Putting down the tray.)* Up and about, that's good.

NIKOLAI: I'm not being nosy.

ILSE: Don't be silly, of course you're not. Here drink your tea while it's still hot.

NIKOLAI: Thank you.

(ILSE pours and hands him his cup.)

ILSE: There, we'll have something to eat later …

NIKOLAI: I can't pay you.

ILSE: There's no need for that.

(They drink. ILSE looks at him. He avoids making eye contact. Pause.)

NIKOLAI: Do you live alone?

ILSE: Yes.

(They sip tea.)

ILSE: I was thinking soup and bread for dinner?

NIKOLAI: Yes.

ILSE: Best to start with something simple, build your strength.

NIKOLAI: I'm not that hungry.

ILSE: Nonsense, I bet you're starving.

NIKOLAI: No.

ILSE: I know they didn't feed you very much …

NIKOLAI: I didn't notice.

ILSE: *(Teasing.)* Don't play games, you look like you're dying of hunger.

(Pause.)

NIKOLAI: I don't feel anything.

(ILSE is taken aback.)

ILSE: Well … after you've eaten you'll feel like new.

NIKOLAI: Like a newborn baby, I'll never be that.

ILSE: *(ILSE doesn't know how to react to such despondency.)* Why don't you have a bath while I get dinner?

NIKOLAI: *(Embarrassed.)* Yes, I'm sorry.

(ILSE puts her teacup on the tray. She looks at a despondent and lost NIKOLAI.)

ILSE: The King rides out every day for an hour, sometimes two. It's a symbol of defiance, resistance. It gives me great hope. You can watch him ride on his white horse; I've nicknamed Snowy, from the bedroom window, take strength from that.

NIKOLAI: I'm not a King.

ILSE: But you must be a survivor.

(The music gets louder as the scene merges into a domestic sequence of activity between ILSE and NIKOLAI. The lights change to suit the various activities and mood. ILSE exits with the tray. NIKOLAI starts to take off his clothes. ILSE enters with a neatly packed set of clothes. As ILSE goes about her chores the music gives way to her singing a song. A lullaby soothes the atmosphere. NIKOLAI changes into them. She takes the old clothes away. He picks up a book and starts to read. He paces about. ILSE enters with a pair of boots and hands them to NIKOLAI, he takes them and leaves. ILSE picks up the receiver of the telephone, dials and speaks but we don't hear her conversation, she hangs up as NIKOLAI enters with a cloth and shoe polish and starts to clean his boots and puts them on. His hair is combed and looks better. ILSE enters with a laundry basket and gets NIKOLAI to help her fold the sheets. He teases her, she laughs. ILSE takes the sheets and exits. NIKOLAI closes the curtains and moves the chair into a corner. The song fades as she stops singing. The scene becomes sombre. NIKOLAI sits and once again his expression is

vacant. ILSE enters in her uniform and little nurse bag, she checks if the uniform is all correct and goes to NIKOLAI, is about to say something but decides to leave him alone. She exits. Night has set in and the room is dimly lit. Silence. Suddenly the phone rings really loudly, piercing across the room.

It startles NIKOLAI, he jumps up; he doesn't know what to do. He wanders about. The phone rings relentlessly and maddening. He can't stand it and answers it.)

NIKOLAI: Hello … yes … no one … hello … trunk call … what? Operator … I don't know … can you hear me … hello …

(ZACK enters talking on the phone. He stands in a single light.)

ZACK: Ilse?

NIKOLAI: No … I don't know …

ZACK: I want to speak to Ilse Paulsen …

NIKOLAI: She's not here …

ZACK: Who is this?

NIKOLAI: What? I don't understand …

(Silence.)

NIKOLAI: Hello … hello … are you there?

ZACK: Is that Valby 6433?

NIKOLAI: Yes, I think so … Valby 6433.

(Brief pause.)

ZACK: Nikolai?

NIKOLAI: Yes …

ZACK: Zack, it's Zack … oh my God … Nik …

NIKOLAI: Zack? Where are you?

ZACK: How are you? Are you alright?

NIKOLAI: Zack?

ZACK: Yes, yes … it's me, how are you?

NIKOLAI: Are you here? Have you come back?

ZACK: No I'm in France …

NIKOLAI: What …?

ZACK: Vichy.

NIKOLAI: What? Where?

ZACK: The Embassy is here, in Vichy, Free France.

NIKOLAI: Free …

ZACK: How are you?

(NIKOLAI gathers his strength before answering.)

NIKOLAI: Fine, I'm doing great?

ZACK: *(Doesn't believe him.)* When did you come home?

NIKOLAI: A week, maybe two …

ZACK: *(Starts to get worried.)* Did Ilse say I was going to call …?

NIKOLAI: No, she's out, working, I think …

ZACK: Are you alright?

NIKOLAI: Yes … *(Softer.)* Yes …

ZACK: You sound strange … did they hurt you …

NIKOLAI: No, no … God no … just questions …

ZACK: Oh, questions … what about the apartment …

NIKOLAI: Home …

ZACK: Yes, your home?

NIKOLAI: They took it …

ZACK: Took it, why?

NIKOLAI: Why?

ZACK: I'm trying to get back; I want to see you ...

(NIKOLAI starts to get emotional.)

NIKOLAI: Oh, no don't ... please ...

ZACK: Why not? I miss you ...

NIKOLAI: Yes ... *(He cries.)*

ZACK: Nikolai, I will be back, I promise ...

NIKOLAI: Promise ...

ZACK: Don't cry, please, I miss you so much ...

NIKOLAI: Miss ... you ... *(He weeps.)*

ZACK: We're still here ... I'll come and get you ...

NIKOLAI: Nothing ...

ZACK: What, I didn't hear you ...

NIKOLAI: I'll wait ...

ZACK: Good, wait for me ...

NIKOLAI: Yes.

(Silence.)

ZACK: Are you still there ...?

NIKOLAI: *(Cries.)* Yes ...

ZACK: I love you ...

NIKOLAI: Love ...

(He lowers the receiver and cries.)

ZACK: Nik ... Nik ... can you hear me ...

(NIKOLAI cries, lifts the receiver, listens then hangs up. ZACK is frantic on the other side, he taps the phone ....)

ZACK: Nik ... Nik ...

(The line has gone dead. ZACK is left, worried, agitated and scared. The light on him fades to black as he exits. NIKOLAI sinks to the floor as he cries and through his tears, pain and anger he lets out a roar. A young man, defeated, ruined and destroyed.)

***   ***   ***

ACT TWO

Music plays. It starts with military marches and then develops into more melodic tunes. A collage of images is screened showing a world about to die. Archive footage, clips and photos are projected randomly across the stage. The Third Reich in its last days as the Allies advance, people scatter, horrors are revealed and the thousand-year dream lies in tatters. The final months of the Second World War are screened as hope, life and safety returns to the people of Europe. OBERGRUPENFUHRER GENERAL HEINRICH VON AESCHELMAN is seated on a wooden chair. He wears only his uniform trousers and a white shirt which hangs loose. He drinks from a bottle of Champagne. He looks lost and alone. DOCTOR CARL PETER VÆRNET enters. He's ill at ease in the GENERAL's quarters. The GENERAL doesn't see him. DOCTOR VÆRNET waits, nothing, he clears his throat …

VÆRNET: You wanted to see me, Heinrich?

GENERAL: *(Turns.)* Ah … there you are … yes …

VÆRNET: Drinking so early?

GENERAL: My drinking is no concern of yours …

VÆRNET: Of course not …

GENERAL: I've received a communiqué from Reichsfuhrer Himmler …

VÆRNET: *(Excited, smiles.)* Oh yes …

GENERAL: He is most displeased.

VÆRNET: Really? May I enquire, why?

GENERAL: Your treatment is not working.

VÆRNET: I may have had problems with some of the inmates but I assure you it's most effective.

GENERAL: On the contrary, it's a disaster.

VÆRNET: Disaster is a harsh word, you must realise every person is different; the therapy must be tailored to each individual …

GENERAL: We do not have the time or the money to keep experimenting. We need quick solutions.

VÆRNET: I'm working as fast as I can, I already treated seventeen inmates.

GENERAL: Two died of infection and the other fifteen are still homosexuals.

VÆRNET: On some people it takes longer to have effect.

GENERAL: Months is long enough.

VÆRNET: But I proved to it worked.

GENERAL: On only ONE patient.

VÆRNET: I will double the dose, I WILL find a solution.

GENERAL: Carl you are a good doctor, your therapies are exemplary but this one is NOT working, I have no choice but to send you back to Copenhagen.

VÆRNET: Back.

GENERAL: It's Reichsfuhrer Himmler's orders. The Third Reich does not need your services anymore.

VÆRNET: Going back, as what?

GENERAL: As before.

VÆRNET: A general practitioner?

GENERAL: That's what you are.

VÆRNET: NO! I create therapies that treat and heal people.

GENERAL: There's nothing stopping you …

VÆRNET: But it's my life's work.

(Silence.)

GENERAL: You need to vacate the apartment by the end of the week.

VÆRNET: So soon …

GENERAL: We don't need you anymore.

VÆRNET: But … but … are you going to help pack, arrange our travel …?

GENERAL: *(Quiet determination.)* By the end of the week!

(DOCTOR VÆRNET is baffled and stunned.)

VÆRNET: So this is what it feels like being abandoned by the Reich.

GENERAL: As long as you live, the Reich will never leave you.

VÆRNET: No, it sticks to you like a bad smell.

(GEORG enters. He's exhausted, tatty and filthy. He ignores the DOCTOR. DOCTOR VÆRNET looks at him, surprised to see him. The GENERAL and DOCTOR VÆRNET glare at each other.)

VÆRNET: Suddenly it makes it all believable.

(He exits. GEORG keeps looking at the GENERAL. The GENERAL turns away.)

GENERAL: What do you want?

GEORG: Is there anything you …

GENERAL: There is nothing.

GEORG: Very well.

GENERAL: Why are you still here?

GEORG: Where am I supposed to go?

GENERAL: Home.

GEORG: I haven't been released yet.

GENERAL: Released? You sound like a convict.

GEORG: Isn't that what I am?

GENERAL: *(Softly.)* Yes.

(Pause.)

GEORG: I'll …

GENERAL: You were always free to try to escape.

GEORG: And as I left you would've had me shot.

GENERAL: You've always been resourceful; I doubt you would've failed.

GEORG: Then what? Where would I go?

GENERAL: Home, waiting for me, you see I want to see you … after the war …

GEORG: After you hang up your uniform?

GENERAL: Yes.

GEORG: … as if in a relationship?

GENERAL: Just so …

GEORG: You have kept me here for over four years …

GENERAL: I needed you.

GEORG: Need or use?

GENERAL: The Allies have the upper hand now, any dreams I had are lost. You can start again. I can visit. We can be together.

GEORG: They won't let you just walk away …

GENERAL: But if you are there, they can't touch me.

GEORG: I won't make any difference at all …

GENERAL: But you will, you can speak …

GEORG: For you?

GENERAL: I treated you well, fed you; bought you everything you wanted …

GEORG: Bribes to cover for you …

GENERAL: They weren't bribes. I wanted to give you all …

GEORG: Like a whore!

GENERAL: You were never that …

GEORG: You never knew how I felt, humiliated, used
             and cheap. *(Pause.)* You never asked me about
             my family, did I have any brothers or sisters,
             where I came from, did I enjoy being with
             you. *(Beat.)* No, every time you finished with
             me you'd kick me away, revelling in your own
             pleasure. It's not how I was taught to love.
             My family were circus players always looking
             out for each other, guarding the ancient
             traditions of performance. I learned my craft
             from watching acrobats, jugglers and clowns
             perform without judgement, jealousy or hate.
             They allowed me to love, my way. Your
             performance is superficial, vacant.

(The GENERAL knows what he says is true and remains silent.)

             When discrimination is whispered behind
             closed doors is when it's at its most dangerous.
             Practised out in the open it's when it's
             most cruel. Given the support, backing and
             encouragement of the state is when it's simply
             savage.

GENERAL: You sound like a politician.

*(The GENERAL drinks. He looks away, humiliated. GEORG looks
at him in disgust.)*

GEORG: I will go, I will re-open my club, my customers
             will return and Copenhagen will once again
             celebrate. *(Beat.)* A forged painting of Da
             Vinci or Chagall or Degas must be burnt but a
             fake person must live with the forgery he has
             created. *(Beat.)* Don't mistake my kindness
             for weakness. I'm kind to everyone but when
             someone is unkind to me, weak is not what
             you'll remember.

(The GENERAL smiles.)

GENERAL: I want to remember you as a beautiful creation.

GEORG: What creation?

GENERAL: You've always been so unkind, never showing me your act.

GEORG: You never bothered to come to see the show at the Corner Light Club. It was such a wasted opportunity, to be surrounded by your kind of people.

GENERAL: It was impossible.

GEORG: You're an Obergruppenfuhrer nothing is impossible.

GENERAL: Show me.

GEORG: Now?

GENERAL: Before it's too late.

GEORG: I'm not prepared.

GENERAL: The Allies are little way off; they won't be here for hours.

GEORG: It may take me hours to get ready.

GENERAL: I don't believe that.

GEORG: I have nothing with me.

GENERAL: I have a box full of items.

GEORG: *(Surprised.)* You have a box?

GENERAL: *(Embarrassed.)* I like to dress up my … my … my friends … *(GEORG laughs.)* What's so funny?

GEORG: You, you're funny.

GENERAL: *(A little angry.)* Funny how?

GEORG: When you're about to be cornered, your secrets are exposed.

GENERAL: It may be your last performance.

GEORG: Oh I doubt that. Go on … *(Waves him on.)* fetch …

(The GENERAL stares at him but knows he has lost power so leaves. GEORG laughs a little but then fear strikes.

These are the most dangerous moments when power is lost and irrational behaviour takes hold. He paces, nervous. The GENERAL enters with a medium-sized box. He hands it to GEORG.)

GENERAL: Use what you need.

(GEORG takes the box, opens it and finds jewellery, lipstick, a couple of wigs and a strange Kimono type outfit. He takes them out one by one.)

GEORG: What a miserly choice.

GENERAL: Work your magic.

(GEORG put on the 'dress', fixes a tatty wig and applies the lipstick. He looks weird, like a freak.)

GEORG: Is this what you like?

GENERAL: Put the necklace on.

(GEORG puts on a pearl necklace.)

GEORG: I've never looked like this before, I feel like a monster.

GENERAL: You can't see what's inside my head.

GEORG: Very well.

(The GENERAL drinks, he sits in semi darkness as GEORG prepares himself.)

GENERAL: Sing for me, for only me.

(Suddenly GEORG has an idea. He smiles and turns away. He sings the freedom song sung throughout Europe in 15 different languages 'CIAO BELLA' GEORG performs in 'drag' with an urgency and determination of a man who smells victory.)

GEORG: One morning I woke up, Ciao Bella, ciao, ciao, ciao. One morning I woke up, and I found an invader, oh partisan, carry me away, Ciao Bella, ciao, ciao, ciao. I feel I'm dying, and if I die, Ciao Bella, ciao, ciao, ciao you'll have to bury me and bury me on the mountain, Ciao Bella, ciao, ciao, ciao under the shadow of a beautiful flower, ciao, ciao, ciao …

and people will pass by and say, oh what a beautiful flower, Ciao Bella, ciao, ciao, ciao and this is the flower of the partisan who died, who died for freedom, Ciao Bella, ciao, ciao, ciao ….

(The GENERAL is in awe but mostly in shock. GEORG stands still, terrified.)

GENERAL: *(Quietly. Disappointed.)* Of all the songs, why that one?

GEORG: The whole world will not stop singing it until we're rid of you.

GENERAL: Can't you show a little kindness?

GEORG: You like a man in a dress because you're too gutless to be who you are.

GENERAL: The last few hours of power are the most dangerous, people become irrational.

GEORG: *(Sings.)* and this flower of the partisan who died, who died for freedom, Ciao Bella, ciao, ciao, ciao …

GENERAL: I need you … to help me …

GEORG: I will not speak for you. Do not count on my protection.

(The GENERAL gets up and goes to GEORG.)

GENERAL: You have no idea what they'll do to me.

GEORG: *(Beat.)* Whatever it is, it'll never be enough.

GENERAL: If they execute me, you'll have blood on your
            hands …

GEORG: And all the blood you spilt is etched on your
            soul.

GENERAL: I can't face it …

GEORG: *(Sings.)* Ciao Bella, ciao, ciao, ciao.

GENERAL: I can't take the pain.

GEORG: Weak to the last.

GENERAL: I'm a lump of jelly squished in your hand.

GEORG: *(Goes to him.)* I'll dribble it down your chest.

GENERAL: and I'll smother it across your mouth.

GEORG: You need to be close to do that.

GENERAL: Yes, really close.

GEORG: Enough to smell the sweet jelly stuck to your
            skin.

GENERAL: It dries like glue.

GEORG: You'll expire before it does.

(GEORG stands very close to the GENERAL.)

GENERAL: Like the last flicker of a dying candle.

GEORG: Just like that.

GENERAL: Without a legacy.

GEORG: There isn't one anyway.

*(GEORG kisses him. The GENERAL doesn't move, he's spellbound,
his body aches with lust. He breaks down, like a coward.)*

GENERAL: How shall I go ….? *(Sings.)* Ciao Bella, ciao,
            ciao, ciao …

GEORG: Cyanide.

GENERAL: There is no honour in that …

GEORG: It's the way of a coward …

(GEORG moves away leaving a defeated GENERAL.)

GENERAL: Then stay with me until it's over.

GEORG: Oh sure, I should sit by your side; hold your hand until you slip away. No!

GERENAL: Why not?

GEORG: Some people deserve to die alone.

GENERAL: Never knew how cruel you could be.

(GEORG gives him a final look, turns and heads out ….)

GEORG: Neither did I?

(GEORG is gone. The GENERAL takes out his wallet, opens it and removes a pill; he closes his hand, takes a swig from the bottle, opens his hand, looks at the pill, cracks it open with a bite and downs it with Champagne … BLACK OUT.

***   ***   ***

BRITISH AND ALLIED HEADQUARTERS.
MAJOR RONALD HEMINGWAY'S OFFICE. 1945.

DOCTOR CARL PETER VÆRNET sits in front of a very utilitarian table.
A bright white light shines making him feel uncomfortable. His suit is
dishevelled and he looks drawn and tired. There is nothing else in the
stark room. DOCTOR VÆRNET looks around. Waits. Silence. He coughs.
Silence. MAJOR RONALD HEMINGWAY, 40s enters, a British Army
Officer in charge of Prisoners of War. He's quite good looking and with
a very efficient manner. He holds a file, goes to the table, pulls the chair
and sits in front of DOCTOR VÆRNET.

HEMINGWAY: Name?

VÆRNET: Carl, Peter Værnet.

HEMINGWAY: What are you doing here?

VÆRNET: I'm not entirely sure …

HEMINGWAY: Why not?

VÆRNET: Well I don't know …

HEMINGWAY: How long have you been in Alsgade Skole
camp?

VÆRNET: About four months.

HEMINGWAY: You're not sure?

VÆRNET: I don't keep track of time.

HEMINGWAY: Why not? Time is what life is made of.

VÆRNET: Indeed.

(HEMINGWAY looks through the file.)

HEMINGWAY: After Britain's liberation of Denmark, and with
the authority of the Danish government, you
will answer to Allied forces.

VÆRNET: I understand.

HEMINGWAY: Your dossier is very sparse.

VÆRNET: I wouldn't know, I didn't write it.

HEMINGWAY: You're answers were very vague at your previous interrogation.

VÆRNET: I was never asked any specific questions.

HEMINGWAY: Why were you arrested?

VÆRNET: Is that not in your dossier?

HEMINGWAY: All the facts are very fluid, nothing sticks or rings true.

VÆRNET: Perhaps it's because I'm an innocent man that has done nothing wrong.

(Pause.)

HEMINGWAY: I find it odd that in Denmark no one likes to talk about the war.

VÆRNET: We are not proud of reaching a compromise with Germany.

HEMINGWAY: *(Sotto Voce.)* Cowards!!!

VÆRNET: That's unfair …

HEMINGWAY: *(Looks at him.)* Where are you from?

VÆRNET: Copenhagen.

HEMINGWAY: Before that.

VÆRNET: Skagen, in Nordjylland.

(HEMINGWAY reads a little further, closes and puts the file down. The two men stare at each other.)

HEMINGWAY: Are you or have you ever been a member of the Nazi party?

VÆRNET: No.

HEMINGWAY: This meeting will be much easier for if you tell me everything.

VÆRNET: No, I have never been a member of the Nazi party.

HEMINGWAY: You were seen wearing a Nazi uniform.

VÆRNET: That is correct.

HEMINGWAY: Then you're a Nazi.

VÆRNET: No, I'm a member of the Danish Nationalist Party.

HEMIGWAY: Same thing.

VÆRNET: You'll find they are very different.

(Pause.)

HEMINGWAY: Where were you based?

VÆRNET: Copenhagen.

HEMINGWAY: And?

VÆRNET: Prague.

HEMINGWAY: And?

VÆRNET: Prague.

(He taps the file.)

HEMINGWAY: Do you deny you worked in Buchenwald?

VÆRNET: No.

HEMINGWAY: Then why didn't you say you were in Buchenwald?

VÆRNET: I answered your question.

HEMINGWAY: No you said Prague.

VÆRNET: And you asked where was I based?

(HEMINGWAY taps quicker.)

HEMINGWAY: Buchenwald was a labour camp?

VÆRNET: That is correct.

HEMINGWAY: Were experiments carried out there?

VÆRNET: No more than in any other facility.

HEMINGWAY: What were you doing in Buchenwald?

VÆRNET: My duty.

HEMINGWAY: In what capacity?

VÆRNET: Doctor.

HEMINGWAY: Are you trying to hide behind the medical profession?

VÆRNET: Not at all, I'm very proud of my profession.

(Pause.)

HEMINGWAY: What do you know of the horrors perpetuated by the Nazi regime?

VÆRNET: Horror is a misleading word. To achieve a new social world order certain measures have to be taken.

HEMINGWAY: Social you say? Social means companionship, a friendly gathering, allowing that to flourish creates a gentle and stable society.

VÆRNET: Providing that society is clean.

HEMINGWAY: Doctor you say?

VÆRNET: Yes.

HEMINGWAY: Did you remove tattooed skin in order to make lampshades?

VÆRNET: No, Doctor Waldemer Hoven was assigned that task.

(MAJOR HEMINGWAY stares at him. His expression turns to disgust. He gets up and walks away.)

HEMINGWAY: We walked into Bergen Belsen as if it was your front gate. No guard, no resistance, nothing. A group of people greeted us. They were normal, a bit dirty for sure, but not ill or malnourished. They were sent as a front, to hide what was behind. We moved forward and I stood onto a puddle; it squelched as if it was something soft. It was rotting flesh. An arm reached out to me, white eyeballs wide, unseeing, in the blood mask that had been a face. A gurgling voice said, 'Help. Kill me.' I continued to walk into hell. *(Beat.)* I lost sight of the time. I couldn't sleep; all I did was work to help people. My commander became concerned and posted me to Copenhagen. It's pleasant and safe, he said. SAFE!!! How? I will not let any of you slip away and I don't play games. *(Pause. He calms down. He goes back to DOCTOR VÆRNET. He stands over him.)* I was sent to identify any war criminals.

VÆRNET: Of which there are many.

HEMINGWAY: To make an assessment of your circumstances I need all the facts.

VÆRNET: I practice an open book policy.

HEMINGWAY: Your dossier states you had a hand in killing inmates at Buchenwald concentration camp, 56,000 died there.

VÆRNET: That is an exaggeration.

HEMINGWAY: You deny it?

VÆRNET: I'm only a General Practitioner.

HEMINGWAY: *(Losing his patience.)* Doctor Værnet did you murder any inmates.

VÆRNET: Murder!!!??? Such a vulgar word, no, I did not.

HEMINGWAY: You have no knowledge of these murders?

VÆRNET: The Third Reich was designed to last for a thousand years; it could not have any form of impurity within its system. All I did was assist in its purification.

HEMINGWAY: *(Disgusted.)* Like filtered water.

VÆRNET: Precisely.

HEMINGWAY: Tell me Doctor, how did you assist in this 'purification'?

VÆRNET: Like any other Doctor; by identifying the disease and ultimately finding a cure.

HEMINGWAY: A cure?

VÆRNET: That's right.

HEMINGWAY: How?

VÆRNET: Apart from curing common ailments I also provided new therapies.

HEMINGWAY: What kind of therapies?

(DOCTOR VÆRNET changes his line of thought.)

VÆRNET: I treated seventeen inmates.

HEMINGWAY: *(Irritated.)* You're not answering my questions. Did these treatments lead to any deaths?

VÆRNET: Two died of infection, that had nothing to do with me.

HEMINGWAY: What were these therapies and treatments?

VÆRNET: I have developed a very successful therapy for the cure of homosexuality.

HEMINGWAY: What? Homosexuality can be cured?

VÆRNET: Certainly. With my testosterone hormone injection all impure thoughts are rapidly removed.

HEMINGWAY: This injection, has been proved to be successful?

VÆRNET: Extremely, after a short time all my patients were rid of that dreaded disease.

HEMINGWAY: Can you prove it.

VÆRNET: I have proved it on many occasions.

HEMINGWAY: If this is true, it's incredible.

(DOCTOR VÆRNET seizes his chance.)

VÆRNET: Oh I assure you, it's quite true.

HEMINGWAY: I've never heard of such a thing.

VÆRNET: When the world is at war, it's very difficult to publicize such ground-breaking findings.

(HEMINGWAY is very impressed.)

HEMINGWAY: Homosexuality is illegal in Britain.

VÆRNET: A very wise policy.

HEMINGWAY: In Britain we practice chemical castration.

VÆRNET: I'm aware of that, it's ineffectual.

HEMINGWAY: With the war these treatments have taken a back seat. They're no longer used as rigorously as before. Britain may be bruised and battered, but it must look to a bright, modern, industrious future. It can't afford to have this stain on its reputation.

VÆRNET: My treatment is very cheap to produce.

HEMINGWAY: Thousands have been given the medication but it makes them ill, unable to work. We can't afford to have them out of the work place.

VÆRNET: All it takes is a simple injection.

HEMINGWAY: *(Thinking.)* Indeed.

VÆRNET: Tell me Major, how come you know so much about this subject?

HEMINGWAY: Knowledge Doctor, knowledge. It was information and knowledge that won us the war, not soldiers or armoury.

VÆRNET: Knowledge indeed, the power of Kings.

HEMINGWAY: Tell me, this treatment, cure, as you call it, would it stand up to scrutiny by the Royal College of Surgeons?

VÆRNET: I have no doubt it will be embraced by such an illustrious institution.

HEMINGWAY: Would you be prepared to present it to all the British medical authorities?

VÆRNET: It would be my honour.

HEMINGWAY: Tell me about the procedure.

VÆRNET: *(Clears his throat.)* It starts with an interrogation. One must ascertain that the individual is indeed a homosexual.

HEMINGWAY: You mean they're devious.

VÆRNET: Extremely Major; you see when the disease takes hold it warps the mind making them chronic liars. My method trips them up very easily. I simply ask them about family, their childhood, any special friends, I make them believe I'm interested which inadvertently makes them reveal the truth.

HEMINGWAY: Ingenious.

VÆRNET: The patient is then strapped onto a bed and I inject the medication.

HEMINGWAY: How?

VÆRNET: One injection in each testicle.

HEMINGWAY: Without an anaesthetic?

VÆRNET: Yes.

HEMINGWAY: That must be incredibly painful.

VÆRNET: I've never found the need for an anaesthetic.

(Pause.)

HEMINGWAY: Go on!

VÆRNET: The molecule is full of strong testosterone hormone which is then released slowly into the system over a short period of time; you see time is of the essence. Once it's fully absorbed the patient is cured.

HEMINGWAY: And you are positive it works.

VÆRNET: Absolutely.

HEMINGWAY: You do realise that the British Medical profession will question and scrutinize your methods down to the very last detail.

VÆRNET: and their conclusion will be that my method works and they will recommend it for general use in Britain, across the Commonwealth and Empire.

HEMINGWAY: *(Thinks.)* The Empire, yes … Can I stake a claim?

VÆRNET: It would be unfair to claim you had a hand in its invention.

HEMINGWAY: Yes … yes … that would be unfair.

VÆRNET: But I would certainly state you were the one who brought it to Britain.

HEMINGWAY: Yes … that would be newsworthy wouldn't it?

VÆRNET: I'll shout the news from every rooftop in London.

(HEMINGWAY gets up and paces about thinking. DOCTOR VÆRNET smiles to himself as he's realized he has a way out. Pause.)

VÆRNET: Does this mean I can leave?

HEMINGWAY: Leave?

VÆRNET: Yes, if there is nothing else …?

HEMINGWAY: I'm deeply moved by this news Doctor. Is there any way you can show me?

VÆRNET: *(Worried.)* Oh I'm not sure; I'd need access to a surgery and a nurse. These are difficult times; such specialized equipment is hard to come by.

HEMINGWAY: Perhaps the forces would help.

VÆRNET: I'm sure they would but aren't they otherwise
            engaged?

HEMINGWAY: Yes … Let me see what I can do.

*(Suddenly DOCTOR VÆRNET becomes worried, he needs another
way out. He thinks fast. Brief pause.)*

VÆRNET: Ah ….yes … ah … Naturally I'm only too
            willing to oblige but … However in my
            condition I need as much rest as possible.

HEMINGWAY: Condition? What condition?

VÆRNET: It's my heart … I suffer from a weak heart.

HEMINGWAY: Can you travel?

VÆRNET: I find travelling a huge strain. I can only
            manage short trips. *(Beat.)* They fear I may not
            have much time left.

HEMINGWAY: Oh my dear man, you should've told me at
            once.

(DOCTOR VÆRNET has cracked it. He's found a way out.)

VÆRNET: Oh I didn't want to impose; besides I was
            unsure of my fate.

HEMINGWAY: But we must help you …

VÆRNET: Oh I could never repay your kindness.

HEMINGWAY: Nonsense, I have found the man that has the
            cure.

VÆRNET: Indeed you have.

HEMINGWAY: Return to the camp for now and I will talk with
            London and we'll find a way to get you over to
            Britain. *(Thinks.)* I'll arrange a flight.

VÆRNET: Oh no, Major, it is not possible for me to fly
            with my weak heart.

HEMINGWAY: I'll arrange a passage on a ship.

VÆRNET: I hear the North Sea has many unexploded bombs and submarines besides I need to rest before I can make such a long journey.

HEMINGWAY: Very well, I'll send you to the country; fresh air will do you good. Help you recover.

VÆRNET: That would be wonderful …

HEMINGWAY: I'll arrange it immediately.

VÆRNET: Except …

HEMINGWAY: Except … what?… what's the matter?

VÆRNET: Well, you see, in Sweden they have a very good, new treatment for a weak heart. It's a course of Vitamin E.

HEMINGWAY: Sweden?

VÆRNET: Yes, it's not far.

HEMINGWAY: But you Danes hate the Swedes.

VÆRNET: Hate is such a vicious word.

HEMINGWAY: Sweden has always been neutral; we have no jurisdiction over there.

VÆRNET: It has always been our trusted friend.

HEMINGWAY: How long will the treatment take?

VÆRNET: Three months.

HEMINGWAY: and after three months you'll be in a position to go to Britain?

VÆRNET: Most certainly …

(HEMINGWAY paces, thinking, excited.)

HEMINGWAY: To allow you to travel, I need evidence. I need an electrocardiogram.

VÆRNET: *(Worried.)* Of course.

HEMINGWAY: I need it as soon as possible.

VÆRNET: My condition is a series of palpitations; they may not register on an electrocardiogram.

HEMINGWAY: Why not.

(DOCTOR VÆRNET's mouth is dry; he's worried; panic sets in. He tries to worm his way out.)

VÆRNET: It's a delicate matter which I doubt modern medicine will discover.

(HEMINGWAY looks at him; he's full of vigour and excitement. Nothing is going to get in the way of his moment. After a moment he speaks.)

HEMINGWAY: I will ask for the result to come to me first. *(Pause.)* I WILL reveal you have a weak heart.

VÆRNET: *(Smiles.)* I understand.

HEMINGWAY: Have you got a place to convalesce? Somewhere in the country perhaps?

VÆRNET: My brother has a farm near Vordingborg.

HEMINGWAY: Excellent. Make arrangements to visit him.

VÆRNET: At once.

HEMINGWAY: Go back to Alsgades Skole for now and I'll get the clearance from London.

VÆRNET: *(As he gets up.)* Certainly.

(HEMINGWAY goes to him, takes his hand and shakes it.)

HEMINGWAY: Together we'll make the front page of *The Times*.

VÆRNET: Yes, *The Times* … we will.

(Suddenly and unexpected ZACK enters. HEMINGWAY is shocked and startled. DOCTOR VÆRNET turns to ZACK.)

HEMINGWAY: Who are you? What do you want?

ZACK: Ah, I'm looking for …

HEMINGWAY: How did you get in?

ZACK: Your secretary told me you were free.

HEMINGWAY: Well I'm not.

VÆRNET: No matter, I was about to leave …

HEMINGWAY: Yes, thank you Doctor.

(HEMINGWAY extends his hand and DOCTOR VÆRNET shakes it.)

ZACK: Ah, a Doctor?

(DOCTOR VÆRNET full of self-importance turns to ZACK.)

VÆRNET: Yes, Doctor Værnet. *(He extends his hand but ZACK does not take it.)*

ZACK: Doctor Værnet, ah yes, I remember you.

VÆRNET: *(Suddenly realises who ZACK is.)* Ah, no, I don't think we've met.

ZACK: Yes, we have, I visited your Surgery.

VÆRNET: I see a lot of patients; I can't be expected to remember everyone.

ZACK: No, no, I'm not one of your patients, I'm …

(DOCTOR VÆRNET cuts him short and turns to the MAJOR.)

VÆRNET: *(Turns to HEMINGWAY.)* You have been very helpful Major thank you.

ZACK: *(Blurts it out.)* I'm looking for someone.

HEMINGWAY: Typical Americans, rude and vulgar.

VÆRNET: *(Ignores HEMINGWAY.)* Who?

ZACK: A friend …

VÆRNET: *(Becomes interested.)* Oh yes … I see … a friend.

ZACK: You wouldn't know him, Nikolai Bergsen.

(Of course DOCTOR VÆRNET knows the name. He stares at ZACK. ZACK feels awkward.)

HEMINGWAY: Leave your details with my secretary …

VÆRNET: Bergsen, a very good, strong Danish name.

ZACK: Yes. *(Beat.)* I believe you met him once.

(DOCTOR VÆRNET stares at ZACK, not knowing what to say turns to the MAJOR.)

VÆRNET: *(As he leaves.)* Good day Major, I await your instructions.

HEMINGWAY: Thank you Doctor …

(DOCTOR VÆRNET exits. ZACK finds him peculiar but presses on.)

ZACK: It's very important I find him.

HEMINGWAY: Every case is important.

ZACK: I work at the American Embassy.

HEMINGWAY: So what? You want special treatment?

ZACK: This is case of national security.

HEMINGWAY: I doubt it.

ZACK: Who do I need to talk to?

HEMINGWAY: Leave all you contact details with my secretary and I will give it priority.

ZACK: That's it?

HEMINGWAY: There are millions of displaced persons in Europe, you're lucky I'm giving yours priority.

ZACK: Is there anywhere else I can try …

HEMINGWAY: The hospital.

ZACK: I've been there …

HEMINGWAY: The police.

ZACK: They referred me to you.

HEMINGWAY: The morgue.

(ZACK is shocked, angry.)

ZACK: Thank you for your help Major.

HEMINGWAY: If he's out there, we will find him.

ZACK: Yes.

(ZACK looks at HEMINGWAY.)

HEMINGWAY: Good day Mr Travis.

ZACK: *(Unimpressed.)* Yeah, so long …

(ZACK glares at him and storms out. HEMINGWAY is irritated, looks down at the file, picks it up and smiles as the lights darken.

***   ***   ***

COPENHAGEN AND MALMO 1946.

The scene splits into two and are lit in different colours and the never cross over. ZACK and ILSE are in COPENHAGEN and DOCTOR VÆRNET and GORAN are in MALMO, SWEDEN. It's cold, dank night. ZACK is waiting. The collar of his coat is turned up. DOCTOR VÆRNET is in semi-darkness in a corner. The night air whistles past them creating an eerie sound. Mist and fog from the Baltic Sea envelope them. GORAN enters looking around. He looks like a very dodgy character. His fedora sits low and shivers. DOCTOR VÆRNET sees him but doesn't approach. ILSE enters. She wears a heavy coat and a hat. She's frightened.

GORAN: Doctor? Doctor Værnet is that you?

VÆRNET: Who sent you?

GORAN: Night owl.

VÆRNET: Who?

GORAN: Night owl.

VÆRNET: Wait.

GORAN: I can't stay long.

VÆRNET: What have you got for me?

GORAN: What you asked for.

VÆRNET: From whom?

(GORAN goes towards DOCTOR VÆRNET as ILSE steps forward.)

ILSE: Hello … Is someone there?

ZACK: Yes.

ILSE: Where are you?

ZACK: Ilse, its Zack.

ILSE: I'm frightened.

ZACK: It's OK, it's me … Zack.

ILSE: Why here, at night?

ZACK: I don't trust anyone.

ILSE:	I'm cold.
GORAN:	Money! I have the money from the British authorities.
VÆRNET:	How much?
GORAN:	It should be enough.
VÆRNET:	I have a family.
GORAN:	There is no more.
VÆRNET:	Who gave it to you?
GORAN:	Don't know, they just told me to hand it over.
VÆRNET:	Give it to me.
GORAN:	No there is too much light.
VÆRNET:	Come here, into the dark.

(The two men move into a darker corner. GORAN takes out an envelope stuffed with money, he holds it.)

ILSE:	This feels so wrong. I feel like a thief.
ZACK:	They're hunting collaborators … any encounter raises suspicions.
ILSE:	It's worse than having the Germans.
ZACK:	Where … where is Nik?
ILSE:	Home.
ZACK:	Which home?
ILSE:	His.
ZACK:	I've been there; he's not there.
ILSE:	I can't say.
ZACK:	You know? Why won't you tell me?
ILSE:	I must go.
ZACK:	Please, I want to see him …

ILSE:	I'm freezing to death.
ZACK:	*(Grabs her.)* Tell me …
GORAN:	They mentioned something about an X-Ray.
VÆRNET:	Yes … yes it's my heart.
GORAN:	The first one was destroyed.
VÆRNET:	Was there another one?
GORAN:	Yes …
VÆRNET:	Yes … yes, of course there was. What did it show?
GORAN:	A chronic heart condition.
VÆRNET:	*(Smiles.)* Good, good.
ILSE:	I promised.
ZACK:	Break your promise, please I'm desperate.
ILSE:	He would never forgive me.
ZACK:	Without us he has nothing.
ILSE:	With you he'll be in pain.
ZACK:	No, I'll sooth him.
ILSE:	I'm going …
ZACK:	You can't … you mustn't …
ILSE:	Even if I told you, he won't see you.
ZACK:	Let me try, please.
ILSE:	It's no use.
ZACK:	*(Realizes.)* He's staying with you, isn't he?
ILSE:	*(Lies.)* No, I haven't seen him …

(ILSE moves away but does not leave. ZACK leaves her be.)

GORAN:	They let you come to Sweden for treatment, now get out. *(He shoves the envelope into DOCTOR*

	VÆRNET's hands.) Take it, go away, leave Sweden immediately.
VÆRNET:	Not without my family.
GORAN:	Leave before the British hand everything over.
VÆRNET:	That'll take time.
GORAN:	You're being treated in SWEDEN, don't you understand!!! Sweden has always been neutral and does not have an extradition treaty with Germany, but Britain has! Take the money and go!!!
VÆRNET:	*(Irritated.)* I know all that, why do you think I'm here. The British believe in me, they'll never …
GORAN:	You risk being prosecuted and put on trial at Nuremberg.
VAERENET:	*(Suddenly really frightened.)* But how can I leave?
GORAN:	Take a boat to Rotterdam.
VÆRNET:	Where to from Rotterdam?
GORAN:	Boat to Lisbon.
VÆRNET:	Why Lisbon?
GORAN:	From there, Turkey, Arabia, the New World, go wherever you want.
VÆRNET:	But my family?
GORAN:	They can meet you in Lisbon, the British have given you enough money for them to travel First Class if you want, set up a home, anything …. Sail away!
VARENET:	Free.
GORAN:	Like a bird.
VÆRNET:	Perfect.

GORAN: I was never here, do you understand, you never saw me or spoke to me.

VÆRNET: You are like the mist in the night.

(GORAN walks away deep into the fog and out of sight. DOCTOR VÆRNET holds the envelope tight, looks at it and smiles with satisfaction.)

VÆRNET: You are my future, you'll make me invincible. God save Britain and good King George.

(He kisses the envelope, puts it in his pocket and with a smile full of glee exits into the night. ILSE and ZACK are still standing apart.)

ZACK: Take me home Ilse.

ILSE: Leave me alone!!!

ZACK: You know I can't do that.

ILSE: This is so wrong.

(ZACK goes to her, takes her arm and pulls her towards him.)

ZACK: It's the only way.

ILSE: I felt, feel ... so guilty, I cried, God knows I cried ...

ZACK: I know. *(He hugs her.)* Please.

(She pulls away and looks at ZACK, she caresses his face. Beat.)

ILSE: He's ... at home.

(ZACK hugs her. The lights change. She exits. The fog and mist lift. The lights change to a warm cosy glow. ZACK is in ILSE's apartment. He takes off his coat; she folds over her arm. ZACK stops her, kisses her on the cheek, she exits.

ZACK looks around, trying to find evidence of NIKOLAI being there. The room is as it's always been, nothing new has been added. He peeps out of the window. NIKOLAI enters. ZACK turns and sees him. NIKOLAI is wearing a worn pair of trousers, tatty shirt and very old cardigan. His hair is messy and he looks haggard and older than his years. ZACK on the other hand is the picture of health, strong,

healthy and dashing. He smiles. NIKOLAI looks away. They stand
awkwardly, not knowing what to say.)

ZACK: Hi.

(NIKOLAI nods.)

ZACK: It's good to see you Nik.

NIKOLAI: Hi.

ZACK: You're looking good.

NIKOLAI: Don't lie! I'm a mess.

ZACK: Wouldn't go that far.

(NIKOLAI moves away, he can't look at him. ZACK can't find the
words.)

NIKOLAI: Are you going back to France?

ZACK: No, I was transferred back here.

NIKOLAI: Copenhagen?

ZACK: Yes.

NIKOLAI: You always liked it here.

ZACK: It looks like it'll be permanent.

NIKOLAI: *(Vague.)* Oh … well …

(NIKOLAI sits; ZACK moves closer.)

ZACK: Did they find out who forged the painting?

NIKOLAI: What painting?

ZACK: The Chagall?

NIKOLAI: What are you talking about?

ZACK: They told me the gallery was being
                    investigated for acquiring a forged Chagall.

NIKOLAI: and you believed them.

ZACK: No, I told them the gallery had a great reputation.

NIKOLAI: It's not your business.

ZACK: Guess not.

NIKOLAI: Leave me alone.

(Not giving up.)

ZACK: So … did they …?

NIKOLAI: Did they what?

ZACK: Find out who forged the painting?

NIKOLAI: *(Loud.)* FUCK the painting, Christ!!!

(NIKOLAI turns away from ZACK. ZACK wanders about, he refuses to leave. Pause.)

ZACK: Did Ilse take care of you?

NIKOLAI: No it was little Red Riding Hood.

ZACK: *(Teasing.)* Did she bring you a basket of goodies.

NIKOLAI: What?

ZACK: You know; Little Red Riding Hood brings a basket of goodies to Grandma.

NIKOLAI: Jesus, you're soft in the head.

(ZACK laughs and moves away, trying to break the ice, to find a way in.)

ZACK: Ilse did a good job, you look great.

NIKOLAI: If it weren't for her, I would've ended up in a ditch.

ZACK: That would never have happened; Denmark look after their people.

NIKOLAI: and it's more than you did.

(ZACK smiles. He knows it's not true. He moves closer.)

ZACK: I believe Georg is going to open the Corner Light Club again.

NIKOLAI: I wouldn't know …

ZACK: Oh … really?

NIKOLAI: I don't go out anymore.

ZACK: You don't see any of the old gang then?

NIKOLAI: There's no point.

ZACK: We should go, it'll be fun; go out, have a few laughs, drinks …

NIKOLAI: *(Snaps.)* I don't drink.

ZACK: It must be boring talking to Ilse all the time.

NIKOLAI: *(Gets up.)* What are you doing?

ZACK: Nothing, I just …

NIKOLAI: You're wasting your time.

ZACK: I've come to see you.

NIKOLAI: Why?

ZACK: Because I want to.

NIKOLAI: To gloat.

ZACK: No, I didn't mean anything, honest …

NIKOLAI: Get out.

ZACK: Aren't you glad I found you.

NIKOLAI: It's been such a long time.

ZACK: Yes. *(He tries to be funny; to lighten the mood.)* There was the little matter of the war: it got in the way.

NIKOLAI: People crossed Siberia to find each other.

CLAUDIO MACOR

ZACK:	I'm not going to feel guilty …
NIKOLAI:	No you Americans never do.
ZACK:	What's that's supposed to mean?
NIKOLAI:	We had fun for a couple of years, that's it. There's nothing for you here.
ZACK:	There's you.
NIKOLAI:	Yeah, well, my priorities have changed.
ZACK:	We have all changed.
NIKOLAI:	Why don't you ship a quarterback over from Ohio and play with him.
ZACK:	I don't want a quarterback from Ohio, I want you.
NIKOLAI:	I'm not for the taking.

(ZACK is surprised by the reaction. He doesn't understand.)

ZACK:	What happened?
NIKOLAI:	You Yanks are so dumb. People are changed by war.
ZACK:	Yeah, maybe, but I don't see why we can't pick up where we left off.
NIKOLAI:	Why? What for?
ZACK:	Because we're good together.
NIKOLAI:	Together!!! How? Where? Christ we are two men. I can't walk you up the aisle; I can't give you a pretty suburban home full of flowers and pressed white sheets.
ZACK:	Why not?
NIKOLAI:	Because they won't let us.
ZACK:	How we live is our affair.

106

NIKOLAI:	The gossip, the awkward glances, nudging each other when we walk by, whisper to each other, hurling insults.
ZACK:	That's bullshit; you know that never happens in Denmark.
NIKOLAI:	Typical. All you Yanks see is the happy ending, Jeannette MacDonald and Nelson Eddy singing off into the sunset.
ZACK:	*(Breaks into song.)* I remember the night Jeannette MacDonald sat in the ruins and sang, and sang, and sang – San Francisco open, your heart …

(ZACK laughs. NIKOLAI is unimpressed and doesn't laugh.)

NIKOLAI:	Jesus, your brain has turned to mush!!!
ZACK:	Oh come on, it's only a movie!
NIKOLAI:	Fuck the movies …
ZACK:	You shouldn't worry about people, if you love someone.
NIKOLAI:	What the do you know about love?
ZACK:	I know how I feel about you.
NIKOLAI:	Yeah, well take those feelings back to your swanky Embassy.

(ZACK won't give up. He moves closer. NIKOLAI is dying, he wants to hug him, love him, but can't.)

ZACK:	What did they do with your home?
NIKOLAI:	Took it.
ZACK:	Why?
NIKOLAI:	Because of me.
ZACK:	That doesn't make sense.

NIKOLAI: No they don't show that in a Hollywood movie.

ZACK: Christ.

NIKOLAI: Yeah, cosy isn't it.

ZACK: We can get our own place, overlooking the sea, maybe?

NIKOLAI: Fantasy.

ZACK: *(Snaps.)* You have no idea what it was like seeing you dragged away. Those Nazi thugs hurled you into a car. It sped away, wheels screeching as I screamed your name, shouting; trying to make them stop. They checked my papers, mumbled some insult and left. Suddenly there was nothing, I was just standing in the middle of the road, alone, panicked. I couldn't believe what just happened; this strange calm around me didn't seem real. My mouth was dry with fear. I asked the Embassy for help but they said they couldn't get involved with a domestic matter. Domestic!!! It was you for Christ's sake, it wasn't domestic, Jesus! *(Beat.)* I searched Top Secret files, trying to find a name, anyone to speak to. I didn't give a damn if I was caught. How could I leave you? It was no use. It was like you had vanished, no one knew anything, no one wanted to say anything. I was living in limbo, agitated. *(Beat.)* Then they scaled back the Embassy and I had to leave. I didn't want to go, but if I stayed I would've been arrested and interrogated. It would've put you at more risk and danger, so I left. Sailing back to America I had a pit in my stomach. All I wanted was to turn the ship back, dive into the ocean, swim back to you. *(Beat.)* Then came Pearl Harbour and America joined the war. Yeah great, thanks to the Japanese all avenues were blocked.

It was as if my hands had been cut off, the frustration and anger was frightening. *(Beat.)* Ilse was all I had, desperate for her to call and one day she did. She had found you, rescued you. The relief was overwhelming; all my muscles ached for days. *(Beat.)* I stayed away, terrified at how you'd react. *(Beat.)* But ... but ... how could I not see you? *(Pause.)* All I ever wanted to do was protect you.

NIKOLAI: Yeah, well, you failed.

ZACK: What's the matter with you, can't we leave the past behind?

NIKOLAI: I don't live in neat little boxes like you. Happy box; sad box; forget everything box.

ZACK: The only box I want is the one with you in it.

NIKOLAI: That box is sealed.

(ZACK is hurt. He finds it all very difficult and strange. NIKOLAI can't look at him. Silence falls heavy on them.)

ZACK: *(Quietly.)* I love you.

(NIKOLAI remains still.)

NIKOLAI: *(Quiet. Determined.)* No, not that ... don't you dare do that ... just go.

ZACK: Not without you.

NIKOLAI: Because of me.

ZACK: Why?

NIKOLAI: Because there is no love here.

ZACK: You're lying.

NIKOLAI: Do me a favour, fuck off!!!

ZACK: Not now that I found you.

NIKOLAI: Please ...

ZACK: I'll go if you come with me.

NIKOLAI: I like being on my own.

ZACK: We're meant to be together, you know that.

NIKOLAI: You just don't get it, do you?

ZACK: NO! What? *(Loud.)* Tell me!

(NIKOLAI can't stand it anymore and finally cracks. He screams out.)

NIKOLAI: I'M NOT A MAN ANYMORE!!!

(ZACK is shocked. He realizes what's happened. A prolonged, shocked silence.)

ZACK: *(Softly.)* You're my man.

(NIKOLAI looks at him and starts to cry. ZACK is shocked. He can't move he just stands and stares at NIKOLAI who is sinking within himself. ZACK rushes over and takes him in his arms. Hugs him.)

NIKOLAI: I can't do anything …

ZACK: We'll see about that.

NIKOLAI: They ruined me.

ZACK: Whatever they did we can fix it.

NIKOLAI: I fought, I thought of you …

ZACK: I know … we'll find someone to help …

NIKOLAI: It's no use …

ZACK: I'll take you to Switzerland, America …

NIKOLAI: There is nothing …

ZACK: I don't believe that.

NIKOLAI: I'll never be the same again.

ZACK: Together we'll fight this.

NIKOLAI: You're young, you need a strong, healthy man …

ZACK: I need you.

NIKOLAI: It's no use.

ZACK: I want you.

(NIKOLAI pushes ZACK away. He's distraught, embarrassed and ashamed. He screams out all his pain, torment and anger.)

NIKOLAI: *(Screams.)* WHY!!!!???

(ZACK reaches out NIKOLAI takes his hand, ZACK pulls him towards him and holds him.)

ZACK: Who did this?

NIKOLAI: Does it matter now?

ZACK: Yes.

NIKOLAI: The Nazis, the Doctor, what's the point.

ZACK: It was that doctor wasn't it?

(NIKOLAI pulls away.)

NIKOLAI: And even if it was, what are you going to do?

ZACK: Bring him to justice, humiliate him; make him pay.

NIKOLAI: How?

ZACK: There are laws.

NIKOLAI: We are homosexuals, shirt lifters, queers, no one cares about us.

ZACK: You're also a human being.

NIKOLAI: We were treated worse than rats.

ZACK: You are a citizen of a Constitutional Monarchy, you have rights.

NIKOLAI: All those fancy, impressive words mean nothing because all he'll get is a slap across his wrists, whereas I ... I'll never change.

ZACK: I promise you, I'll find him, give him what he deserves and whatever he did to you I will fix it, we'll go to psychologists, surgeons, anyone who'll listen and help, as God is my witness, I'll fix it.

NIKOLAI: Your promises don't hold; you never took me away.

ZACK: I came back, didn't I?

(NIKOLAI cries quietly as ZACK goes to him and takes him in his arms.)

ZACK: They'll never take you again. *(Their world is altered, different but together.)* Never!!!

NIKOLAI: Bullshit.

ZACK: *(Smiles.)* When I'm done I'll take you to Florida, Cuba, Morocco anywhere.

NIKOLAI: Why not home?

ZACK: *(Smiles and kisses him.)* Yes … of course … home is perfect.

(The effects of a cruel and savage treatment are etched on NIKOLAI's face. ZACK kisses him passionately. ZACK breaks away.)

ZACK: You'll never be alone … *(Kisses his cheek.)* You are the love of …

(NIKOLAI grabs him and holds him as he cries. ZACK gently releases him and leads him out. The lights follow them out and change to a bright sunny day.)

***   ***   ***

BUENOS AIRES. 1947. THE PALACE OF CONGRESS.

RODOLFO FREUDE enters. He's full of brio and very excited. He holds a file. He's immaculately dressed and camp. He appears to be more of a maître'd than a government official. He's in a right flap, not knowing which way to turn. RODRIGO, a waiter enters and sets up a table for drinks. He lays out the white tablecloth, positions a couple of glasses and a Champagne ice bucket. He exits. FREUDE calls out …

FREUDE: Consuelo he's not here …. *(No answer.)*
            You did say the Grand Hall … *(Still no
            answer.)* Consuelo cerida are you ignoring me?
            (Nothing.) Oh these girls will be the death of
            me … *(He makes to leave in a flap.)*

(DOCTOR CARLOS PIETRO VARTEN enters. FREUDE sees him.)

FREUDE: Are you the Doctor I've been looking for by
            any chance?

VARTEN: Yes.

FREUDE: Ah, at last, my secretary Consuelo, told me
            you'd be waiting in the Grand Hall. Never
            mind, you're here now, delighted to meet you.
            I'm Rodolfo Freude assistant to the assistant to
            the assistant of the Minister of the Interior.

VARTEN: *(A bit confused.)* How do you do.

(They shake hands.)

FREUDE: My, my what a strong grip you have. Welcome
            … welcome …

VARTEN: Thank you Herr Freude …

FREUDE: Oh no, no, we are in Argentina, it's Señor Freude.

VARTEN: Of course.

FREUDE: I see you changed your name to Doctor Carlos
            Pietro Varten.

VARTEN: Yes, I thought it appropriate.

FREUDE: Makes it sound more local doesn't it?

VARTEN: Indeed.

FREUDE: I work for the Ministry of the Interior.

VARTEN: Yes, I'm aware of that.

FREUDE: Are you settling in well?

VARTEN: Yes my wife and children seem to like it here.

FREUDE: Good, good …

VARTEN: My wife is learning the language, I on the other hand …

FREUDE: Oh not at all … not at all … your Castigliano is very good indeed.

VARTEN: Thank you.

FREUDE: Do you have enough money?

VARTEN: Yes the British authorities have given me ample funds for now.

FREUDE: Marvellous … delighted; don't be shy to ask if you need more.

VARTEN: How very generous.

FREUDE: The government has read with great interest all about your therapies.

VARTEN: Oh really, good.

FREUDE: El Jefa Espiritual de la Nacion, Eva Duarte de Peron.

VARTEN: *(Amazed.)* Evita?

FREUDE: Yes, Evita; The Spiritual Leader of the Nation … darling girl … she expresses her regret she can't be here in person …

VARTEN: Oh there is no need …

FREUDE: Unfortunately a shipment of Salvatore Ferragamo shoes arrived this morning together with Christian Dior's New Look collection, can you imagine! All at the same time! Poor girl she doesn't know which way to turn. They need her immediate attention.

VARTEN: Of course, I understand.

FREUDE: And if that's not all, her maid; that stupid Carmensitta, has misplaced her diamond and ruby encrusted shoe horn …

VARTEN: I'm sure it's somewhere …

FREUDE: It's the one Bulgari designed especially for Evita.

VARTEN: Then I have no doubt they'll find it.

FREUDE: I've already said a little prayer.

VARTEN: Your prayer will be a great comfort to the First Lady.

FREUDE: Oh I do hope so.

(An awkward pause. Neither men know what to say or do. FREUDE smiles.)

VARTEN: *(Quietly.)* I … I … um … I understand that Monsieur Dior is also an undesirable.

FREUDE: *(Sighs.)* Alas yes, but his designs fulfil all of the First Lady's desires.

VARTEN: Undoubtedly.

FREUDE: It was only yesterday that she was telling me that the Peron Government would like you to continue developing your therapies.

VARTEN: That is most kind.

FREUDE: You will have access to any medical facility you require and all the funding you need to achieve a successful result.

VARTEN:	Such generosity can only be repaid with success.
FREUDE:	President Peron's interest is in your cure of those poor unfortunate men.
VARTEN:	Homosexuals.
FREUDE:	*(Shudders.)* Oh that word, it's too horrible to utter.
VARTEN:	My cure is the answer.
FREUDE:	Indeed it is ...

(FREUDE claps his hands and RODRIGO enters with a tray full of Champagne cocktails with umbrellas and cherries, all rather over the top.)

FREUDE:	Have you requested a visa to return to Denmark?
VARTEN:	No, I didn't think a visa was necessary. I wrote to the Danish authorities asking if I would be allowed home.
FREUDE:	Did they reply?
VARTEN:	Yes, they said they couldn't guarantee my safety.
FREUDE:	A very common response, it means you can't return, no matter, Argentina does not have an extradition treaty with Denmark.
VARTEN:	I'm aware of that ...
FREUDE:	You must think of Buenos Aires as your new home ....
VARTEN:	I'm very happy to be here ...
FREUDE:	To make you feel more at home perhaps you could accompany me to the Opera, tonight.
VARTEN:	Opera?

FREUDE: Yes, Madame Elisabeth Schwarzkoph is appearing at the Teatro Colon.

VARTEN: Really?

FREUDE: Yes, in Der Rosenkavalier.

VARTEN: I see.

FREUDE: She'll delight all our new German friends.

VARTEN: *(Not excited at all.)* Enchanting. *(He moves away.)*

FREUDE: *(Suddenly oblivious of the Doctor, to himself.)* Perhaps I can snatch a brief audience with Evita, if she's not drowning in tissue paper and boxes … and maybe grab a peek at the collection, oh it's so exciting.

(Turns and sees the Doctor.) Yes … well … ah look … they've brought Champagne cocktails, *(not impressed.)* How lovely … as a welcome drink … um, yes!

VARTEN: Thank you. I'm honoured.

FREUDE: Indeed you are, looking forward to seeing you at the Opera House tonight.

VARTEN: *(Raises his glass.)* Salute!

FREUDE: Yes … there's that!

(He exits quickly. DOCTOR VARTEN looks around, downs his drink and takes another glass. He sits and drinks, smiles, smug, victorious. The light fades as DOCTOR VARTEN sips. NIKOLAI and ZACK enter.)

ZACK: Doctor Carl Peter Værnet used his son, Kjeld, to request a safe passage back to Denmark on two further occasions.

NIKOLAI: Both requests stated they could not guarantee his safety.

ZACK: He never returned to Denmark.

NIKOLAI: He remained in Argentina.

ZACK: Never hounded …

NIKOLAI: Never prosecuted.

ZACK: And never on any Most Wanted List!

(DOCTOR CARL PETER VÆRNET downs his champagne cocktail, wipes his mouth, smiles and full of pomp exits. NIKOLAI and ZACK watch him leave as they remain alone in a single light.)

NIKOLAI: He died at home on the 25th of November 1965 at the age of seventy-two …

ZACK: With his wife and six children by his side.

ZACK: To this day the British …

NIKOLAI: … and Danish governments have never apologised …

ZACK: … for allowing a Nazi War Criminal to slip away.

NIKOLAI: He ruined hundreds of lives.

ZACK: He remains the forgotten Nazi War Criminal that escaped justice.

(Beat.)

NIKOLAI: His methods have inspired many to experiment and find cures across the world to this very day.

(Pause.)

ZACK: His belief was simply *(Beat.)* SAVAGE.

(NIKOLAI looks at ZACK.)

NIKOLAI: A rose will always be a … rose.

(ZACK goes to NIKOLAI hugs him tightly. NIKOLAI breaks away and puts his arm around ZACK's shoulder and they walk away, together, resolute, happy in love.

Music plays as the lights fade to BLACK OUT.)

THE END.

WWW.OBERONBOOKS.COM